Lake Constance

Table of Contents

Welcome to the "Swabian Sea"

This tour guide offers brief descriptions of all those places on Lake Constance and in the immediate vicinity that are especially worth visiting. It includes localities on the Upper Rhine all the way to Schaffhausen and the famous Rhine Falls.

The total length of the Lake Constance shoreline is 273 km. The largest part of the shoreline (173 km) is in Germany. The Swiss section is 72 km long, the Austrian section 28 km. Due to the relatively long distances and the multitude of holiday resorts, it is advisable to reconnoitre this shoreline strip and its rich landscape and culture in several stages. To avoid the heavy automobile traffic that is often present in the summer months on the lakeside roads, visitors should cover short distances on foot or by bicycle. When it comes to longer distances, visitors should take advantage of the numerous possibilities for travelling by ship. There are more than forty landings to choose from in the Lake Constance / Upper Rhine area. Thirty-five passenger ships and two ferries offer passage for 19,000 persons at

one time. The schedules of the four shipping companies are co-ordinated, thus ensuring optimal connections.

The Lake Constance tour described in this guide begins in Meersburg, one of the strongholds of tourism. Part I, in which the numbers representing the towns are marked in red, leads clockwise around the Übersee or "Upper Lake". The Upper Lake is 46 km long (Constance - Bregenz), 14 km wide (Friedrichshafen-Arbon) and has an area of 500 square kilometres, which definitely makes it the largest section of the lake. Besides Meersburg at the start and Constance at the end, the historic city centre in Lindau is one of the special highlights for tourists. Part II of the tour, which is marked in yellow, covers the approx. 50 km around that section of the lake known in German as the Überlinger See. This section of shoreline, which extends from Mainau Island to Überlingen to Uhldingen-Mühlhofen, is known for its Pile Dwelling Museum. Part III, the one with the green code numbers, describes the little bay known as the Lower Lake, including Reichenau

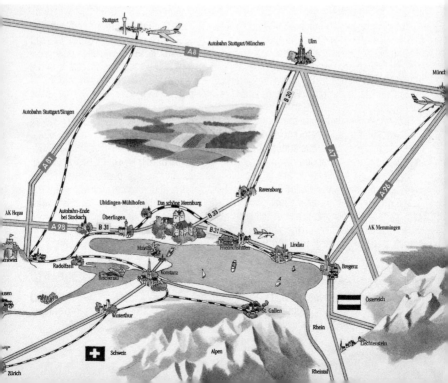

Island, Radolfzell, and the Höri Peninsula, as well as the famous Swiss tourist spots Stein am Rhine and Schaffhausen (with the Rhine Falls), which are part of the Upper Rhine region. Besides places that are directly on Lake Constance, we refer repeatedly to sights and especially pleasant vantage points in the immediate vicinity: the Rhine Valley upstream to Liechtenstein, the Abbey of St. Gall, and Salem, outlooks on the Gehrenberg, Pfänder, Säntis, and Hohentwiel mountains, wildlife protection areas near Eskirch, in the Rhine delta, and in the reed marshes in Wollmattingen and Ermattingen. Lake Constance was created in its present form some 15,000 years ago, during the last ice age, when the enormous Rhine glacier excavated the Lake Constance basin (which is still up to 254 m deep in places). At the northern edge of the glacier, the scree in the end moraine piled up to form the long ranges of hills known as Drumlins today. They, for example, form the Bodanrück between the Überlinger See and the Lower Lake, the hinterland of Lindau, and the hills on the island of Reichenau. The numerous little lakes and moors near Lake Constance were also created by the melting glacier.

Today the lake, which holds 48,500 cubic metres of water, is Central Europe's largest potable water reservoir, supplying water not only to the nearby towns, but to practically the whole of Southern Germany all the way to the Main River. In addition, however, it is one of Germany's most visited travel destinations, thanks to its prime location in a climate known for its mildness and the numerous cultural treasures that have been handed down there.

The vineyards and orchards are famous, especially those on the North Shore. On clear days, the hills there offer a magnificent view of the Alpine panorama across the lake to the South. The gardens, on the other hand, provide guests with fresh fruit and vegetables, aromatic fruit brandies, and full-bodied wine. The main varietals grown in the southernmost wine-growing regions of Germany are the strong-flavoured Müller-Thurgau and the pleasant late Burgundies, which include Red Burgundy (a velvety red wine) and Weißherbst (rosé, a fragrant, light red wine). On Lake Constance, this is often served with fish. While the types of fish that are most important to restaurants are raised almost entirely in the State Hatcheries, they are soon released into the lake to mature under natural conditions. Local favourites include whitefish or Felchen (known in Bavaria as "Renke"), perch (which goes by the name of "Kretzer" or "Egli" here and is the most popular Lake Constance fish), salmon (or Rheinsalm), eel, grayling, trout, pike, arctic charr or Saibling, turbot, catfish, or pikeperch. Whether fried, broiled or boiled, the most important criterion for gourmets is whether the fish is from the freezer chest, a hatchery, or the day's catch on Lake Constance. The difference in taste is considerable, so asking about the origin of the fish is one way of avoiding many disappointments. If you don't trust what you hear or you just don't like fish, it is best to stick to game, the handmade noodles and noodle pockets known as Spätzle and Maul-taschen respectively, Geschnetzeltes and Swiss potato pancakes or Rösti, specialities of Swabian and Swiss cuisine.

Water sports enthusiasts should note that waves on the Upper Lake can reach heights of up to 1.5 m during storms. Otherwise, the water level fluctuates between its high mark in summer and a low mark of approx. 2 m, which is particularly noticeable in the reeded areas. This is due primarily to thaws in the Alps. The water released by these thaws, which continue until mid-summer, mostly flows to Lake Constance by way of the Rhine. On the whole, the Rhine accounts for approx. 70% of the total influx of approx. 10 billion m^3 per year (320 m^3 per hour). Another interesting phenomenon is the curvature of the water level due to the curvature of the Earth's surface. Between Constance and Bregenz, a distance of 46 km, the curvature is still 41.5 m, making it impossible to see from one shore to the other even on the clearest of days.

We hope that this little book will provide you with some interesting information about your vacation area and help you experience a relaxing and yet informative holiday on the "Swabian Sea".

Grüßgott, Servus, Grüezi

Why not spend your holidays at Lake Constance for once? Join the "White Fleet" on an expedition. The only way to really get to know Lake Constance and the Rhine is to experience them, in the truest sense of the word. Sitting on the sun deck, taking a deep breath, and cast off your cares. Relaxation for young and old. Come join us on our attractive cruises. There is virtually no easier or more convenient way to reach the loveliest spots on Lake Constance and the Rhine.

We travel daily to the most famous destinations. In addition, we offer excursions, tours, and all-day cruises between Germany, Switzerland, and Austria. On the weekend, you can dance and party on the ship until late in the night. Or reserve one of our other great trips. From the international starlight cruise to the afternoon cruises during Advent, they are the highpoints of the season.

No matter what you choose, there is a special experience waiting just for you: we promise. Get a whiff of fresh breeze. Bask in the sun, the calmness, and the jovial company.

There is certainly enough room, especially where children are concerned. The food is good, and it's a good thing, too. For as everyone knows, fresh lake air is good for your appetite, Whether a small snack or a buffet for magnificent celebrations: our onboard restaurant will fulfil your every wish. By the way, if you want to share this "lake experience" with friends or colleagues, no problem. Whether for weddings birthdays, company parties or conferences, just a ship from the "White Fleet".

A very proud fleet, with 15 comfortable ships at present, an hourly ferry connection from Germany (Friedrichshafen) to Switzerland (Romanshorn) for passengers, cars, and trucks, and a motor boat. Our experienced skippers will get you to where you are going with minimum hectic and maximum safety.

Numerous special offers, such as the Lake Constance Pass, family tickets, all-day tickets, and special fares for bicyclists make travel on Lake Constance more affordable. It is certainly worth it.

We wish you a shipboard experience that truly crosses all frontiers.

Bodensee-Schiffsbetriebe GmbH
Hafenstraße 6 · 78462 Konstanz
Tel. 07531/281-398 · Fax 281-373
e-mail: info@bsb-online.com
internet: www.bsb-online.com

A pleasant day on Lake Constance

1 MS Graf Zeppelin
2 Ships passing in Meersburg Harbour
3 Starlight cruise
4 Entrance to Lindau Harbour
5 Panorama cruise against the backdrop of the Swiss Alps
6 Evening atmosphere on the lake

BSB
Die Erlebnis-Flotte

Meersburg

Where the Upper Lake meets that part of Lake Constance which is known in German as the Überlinger See - directly opposite Constance - lies one of the most charming towns on Lake Constance: Meersburg (population 5000). The main structure of the Old Palace probably dates back to the 7th century. The former fishing village in the area of the present-day lower town was granted the status of a city in 1299. Meersburg reached the zenith of its importance starting in 1526, when the bishops of Constance - driven away from their traditional residence by the Reformation - chose it as

Meersburg on Lake Constance with the Upper Town Gate, the New Palace (at left) and the massive Dagobertsturm of the Old Palace; the Swiss shoreline is visible in the background.

Spa and Tourism Administration, Kirchstrasse 4, D-88709 Meersburg
Phone: 07532/4311-11 or -10, Fax: 431120, e-mail: info@meersburg.de
Old Palace: Mar. 1 - Oct. 31, 9:00 AM - 6:30 PM daily, Nov. 1 - Feb. 28, 10:00 AM - 6:00 PM daily. **The New Palace and the Dornier Museum:** March 21 - Oct. 31, 10:00 AM - 1:00 PM and 2:00 PM - 6:00 PM daily.
Viticulture Museum: *April - October, Tuesday, Friday, Sunday from 2:00 - 5:00 PM.*
"Fürstenhäusle" Droste Museum: Easter through end-October, 10:00 AM - 12:30 PM daily, and 2:00 - 5:00 PM, Sundays and holidays from 2:00 - 5:00 PM. **German Newspaper Museum:** *April - October, visiting hours: see notice.* **Town Museum:** *Sunday 10:00 AM - 6:00 PM.*
Bible Gallery: *mid-April through October, Tuesday-Sunday 11:00 AM-1:00 PM and 2:00-5:00 PM, closed Mondays, free admission on Sunday.*

their new place of residence and seat of administration. Meersburg's most magnificent era lasted until Napoleon dissolved all ecclesiastical territories in 1803.

Visitors can get the best view of the town from the lake: silhouetted against the sky, the town church can be seen to the left, then the massive Dagobert's Tower and the other buildings of the Old Palace, the Baroque New Palace and, finally, the sprawling facades of the state winery and the former seminary above the sloping vineyards. The "Känzele" between these two provides a beautiful vantage point from which to look out over Lake Constance. The hotels "Wilder Mann" and "Zum Schiff", to the left, form the counterpoints to the lovely staggered gables of the Gredhaus, which formerly served as a granary. This is adjoined on the right by the docks of the German Rail harbour and the boat harbour, further out are the outdoor public swimming pool and the harbour for sailboats.

In front of the **Gredhaus** (1505), the spa ships put ashore and put off from shore bound for Constance, Mainau, Überlingen, Friedrichshafen, Lindau, and Bregenz (tickets available in Gredhaus). This is also where we will begin a walking tour of the sights in town, first of all leading along the well-groomed lakeside promenade. The corner building, now the Hotel "Zum Schiff", was once the chapter court of the cathedral chapter of Constance. At the point where the lake promenade widens into Bismarckplatz, you can see the Unterstadttor (i.e. "Lower Town Gate", also known as the Seetor, i.e. "Lake Gate"), a remnant of the town fortifications, which forms the entrance to Unterstadtstrasse. After just a few metres, we reach the building housing the Winegrowers' Association, which serves as a reminder of the centuries-old winegrowing tradition, as do the other high buildings with their deep

Meersburg: the enormous Gredhaus at the landing place for ships.

cellars. Hidden away close to the gate and set back from the row of houses is the Unterstadtkapelle (i.e. "Lower Town Chapel"). Erected in 1390 as a castle chapel, it was renovated and painted in the 16th century. The elaborately carved Gothic altars are worth seeing (15th cent.).

Outside the town gate, we keep right and walk just a few meters up to the **Altes Schloss** ("Old Palace"). Although no documentary mention of it was made until 1113, the main structure is significantly older than that. Researchers assume that the Merovingian King Dagobert - after whom the mighty tower was named - had the initial fortifications built here in the 7th century, which the succeeding Carolingians maintained as a royal and imperial palace. In 1268, after passing from the Guelfs to the Hohenstaufens, the castle landed in the hands of the prince-bishops of Constance, who used it as a summer

Meersburg: Altar of the Annunciation (1520) in the Lower Town Chapel.

8

Meersburg: Unterstadtstrasse and the Lower Town Gate.

Meersburg: Enchauting blossoms in front of the Old Castle. Poetess Annette von Droste-Hülshoff used the castle as her Lake Constance home from 1841 until her death in 1848.

Meersburg, Old Palace: Annette von Droste-Hülshoff.

Schloss (i.e. "New Palace"), until the end of their temporal rule in 1803. The Altes Schloss was state property for a short time, before being purchased in 1838 by Baron Joseph von Lassberg, the brother-in-law of the poetess Annette von Droste-Hülshoff (1797-1848). It is still in private hands to this day. However, more than 30 of the furnished rooms can be viewed all year round, even without a tour guide. Besides the palace, the castle kitchen, the castle chapel, the princes hall, the armoury, the dungeon, the castle garden, and the battlements, the study of Annette von Droste-Hülshoff ("Die Judenbuche") in the round tower and the room where she died are all open for public viewing. In honour of the 200th anniversary of the poetess' birth and 150th anniversary of her death (1997/98), there will be special guided Droste tours. Medieval chests and wardrobes as well

retreat and, from 1526 on, as a residence. In 1750, they moved to the feudal Neues

Meersburg, Old Palace: room where Annette von Droste-Hülshoff died.

▲ *The poetess' study.*

▲ *The Armoury.*

*Meersburg,
Old Palace:
hall in palace
(ca. 1330).*

▼ *Knights' Hall (13th cen.).*

Gatehouse (16th cen.) with late Gothic crucifix. ▼

as suits of armour, helmets, maces, morning stars, and axes bear witness to the function of the castle in times past. Regularly held recitals featuring medieval music performed on historic instruments, give guests the feeling of being back in that period.

Having arrived at the Altes Schloss, we are now in the Upper Town, which is built upon Tertiary molasse rock.

At the Bärenbrunnen (i.e., "Bear Fountain"), we are back at Steigstrasse, which we can now follow uphill. To the right, there is the rather unimposing former Herdersches Haus, which belonged to the founder of the Herder Publishing House (1801), opposite stands the lovely half-timbered structure of the Lochnerhaus. Below this impressive facade of historic half-timbered houses, the Winzergasse leads us to a small square with the "Schnabelgierebrunnen", a donation of the Shrovetide Fools' Guild. A few artists and artisans have taken up shop in this lane, attracted by the incomparable romantic flair of the Old Town.

There is a set of stairs leading up to the square in front of the town church. The town has its tourist office to the right in the buildings of the Altes Kloster (i.e. "Old Cloister"), a former Dominican convent. Other rooms of the cloister house the Bible gallery. The museum has a unique experiential exhibition, successfully combining exhibits on the world of the Bible as well as the Gutenberg printing press (with printing demonstrations) and the computer (quiz). The town museum is also located on Kirchstrasse, which opens onto Marktplatz nearby. The town muse-

Meersburg: historic half-timbered patrician houses along Steigstrasse. The bay window of the Hotel "Zum Bären" and the Upper Gate are visible at the far right.

Meersburg: Marktplatz with the romantically ivy-wreathed bay windows of the Hotel "Zum Bären" and the Upper Gate, one of the most famous cityscapes on Lake Constance.

13

um contains a collection on the political and artistic history of Meersburg. Among the most impressive of the historic patrician houses are the hotels "Zum Löwen" and "Zum Bären", whose romantic bay windows - with the Obertor in the background - are one of the most well-known scenes from German towns.

Outside the Stadttor (i.e. "Town Gate), Stettener Strasse leads to the right in the direction of Friedrichshafen. A romantic garden house, which can be reached via a reinforced stairway, towers above the vineyard. To this day, it is named "Fürstenhäusle" after its former owners, the prince-bishops of Constance. Annette von Droste-Hülshoff purchased the property in 1843 and gathered inspiration from the splendid view of the lake. The "Droste Museum" is located in the house. A tour takes you through the 6 rooms (incl. the "Parade-zimmer" and "Schwalbennest"), which all contain the furniture of the poetess and her family. Original manuscripts and silhouettes, paintings and jewellery, porcelain and specimens from the poetess' collection of minerals keep her memory alive.

The Meersburg cemetery is situated up above the Fürstenhäusle. To get there, go back down Stettener Strasse, then about 10 minutes right on Mesmerstrasse. Besides the Gothic chapel with its old carved altars, visitors to this place can also see the graves of Annette von Droste-Hülshoff, her brother-in-law, Baron von Lassberg, and Franz Anton Mesmer, who studied magnetic fields in animals and humans. On our way back from the cemetery, let's turn right onto Von-Lassberg-Strasse. We soon arrive at Friedrichshöhe, one of the most beautiful vantage points for viewing the Old Town and lake from above. The set of stairs we just passed takes us back to Mesmerstrasse and Old Town, where we reach the Marktplatz once again through the Obertor. From the Marktplatz, go through the Falbentor beneath the city hall (1551). The Rotscher Hof is standing on your right and the former Schussenrieder Hof on your left: both of these are historical buildings from the period of rule of the prince-bishops. The romantic Vorburggasse begins below the Schussenrieder Hof. The house where Franz Anton Mesmer died is located on this lane. The house is now the home of a viticulture museum, whose special attractions include a mighty "Torkel" (winepress) and the gigantic "Türkenfaß" (50,160 l). Wine-tasting sessions can be arranged for groups here and at the Winegrowers' Association, at the state winery and at the "Haus der Guten Weine" (at Schützenstr. 1) (see info box).

The lane once again leads into the Schlossplatz at the historic "Rotes Haus". A local press historian established the Deutsches Zeitungsmuseum (i.e. "German Newspaper Museum") here. It documents German-lan-

Meersburg: central structure of the New Palace facing Schlossplatz.

guage newspaper history with a presentation of all aspects of production, from paper making to news reporting, everyday editorial work and distribution. The Zeppelin Museum (Schlossplatz 8) also owes its existence to a private initiative. Aside from model airships, the museum also displays the uniforms worn, including the famous light metal caps.

The broad facade of the Neues Schloss forms the southern boundary of the square. Construction of the New Palace

Meersburg, New Palace: Baroque staircase designed by the famous architect Balthasar Neumann.

began around 1712 and was completed in 1740 according to the plans of the famous Baroque architect Balthasar Neumann. It was renovated already between 1759 and 1762. After all, it served as the residence palace of the prince-bishops of Constance from that time until 1802. The living quarters can still be viewed in part to this day as part of a tour. The tour is worth taking just to see the impressive staircase - with wrought iron lattices and magnificent frescoes. After a varied history in the possession of the state of Baden (by turns, the building was used as a state prison, a boarding school for girls, a barracks, a seamen's school, a home for the deaf and dumb, a secondary school and then as a barracks again), the town leases these rooms and makes them available mostly for museum purposes, the remaining great halls on the ground floor serve as facilities for conferences, conventions and social functions. Aside from the aforementioned living quarters of the prince-bishops, which visitors get to see in their original condition, the complex also presently houses the town painting gallery and a Dornier Museum on the history of aviation - especial-

ly of the Dornier Works in Friedrichshafen and the founder of the company. On display in the exhibit are original parts and photos as well as models of the planes, incl. the legendary seaplanes. Visitors are afforded a very nice all-round view of Meersburg's Lower Town and Lake Constance from the sprawling palace terrace. The former palace chapel in the east wing is presently used as a Protestant church. Its harmonious stucco work (by Joseph Anton Feuchtmayer) and the imaginative frescoes are especially delightful to behold. Another pleasing sight is the lovely corbie gable of the former court apothecary at the south-west corner of the palace square. This is where the Höllgasse begins, where a number of lovely facades make quite an impression; outstanding among them, the fabulously entwined facade of the "Winzerstube zum Becher". From the lower area of the Höllgasse, we take one last glance at the old, grey structure of the gate of the Altes Schloss with its wooden bridge and the monument to its most famous inhabitant, before leaving the Upper Town by way of Burgweg. The first thing we pass in the man-made

Meersburg, New Palace: model of the famous Do X jumbo flying boat (1929) in the Dornier Museum.

Meersburg: a view of Lake Constance from the palace terrace.

gorge below the stronghold is the Schlossmühle (i.e. "Palace Mill"). It was built in 1620. Visitors to the town can marvel at its overshot water wheel with a diameter of 8.5 m. It is the largest of its kind in Germany. Passing below the wooden bridge, which was originally constructed as a drawbridge, we gradually descend to the level of Lake Constance, stopping again and again in awe to take in the view of the sparkling lake. The stairs end close to the tourist agency at the Unterstadtstrasse - this is where the accommodation referral service is located for all the accommodations in Meersburg. The extension of the Unterstadtstrasse is the lakeside promenade, which is a path leading to the next town on the lake, Hagnau. Almost any and all kinds of recreational facilities a water-sports enthusiast could hope for are integrated into this area: there are boats for hire and docks for passenger ships, a heated outdoor pool with thermal pools (33° C) and a chance to swim in the clear waters of Lake Constance, berths for windsurfers, a sailboat harbour with sailboats for hire and a yachting school and yachting harbour, in addition to a miniature golf and an exercise area for "landlubbers". Vineyards cover the slopes, stoking the anticipation of the evening twilight hour in one of the hospitable restaurants where visitors can wrap up an eventful day with fine Meersburger Müller-Thurgau or Spätburgunder Weissherbst, with whitefish or Egli (Lake Constance perch) accompanied by fresh vegetables in a relaxed atmosphere.

From Meersburg, it is worth making a short side-trip to the "interior" in the direction of Markdorf (B 33, 5 km). Along the way, we first make a short stop in the district of Ittendorf, where we can view the staggered gable facade of the palace and the Catholic parish church of St. Martin's or pay a visit to the informative Exhibit of Minerals and Fossils. The three medieval peel towers (13th cent.) are distinctive of the townscape here, as is the palace of the bishops of Constance (14th/16th/18th cent., a summer residence at one time) and the former collegiate church of St. Nikolaus (13th/14th cent.) with Baroque additions and a valuable cloaked Madonna (ca. 1470). An hour's walk (or less if you take the car part of the way) away is Markdorf's own mountain, the Gehrenberg. Its summit (754 m above sea level) affords a fantastic view of the Alps on clear days.

Hagnau

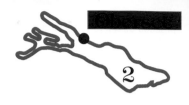

The idyllic winegrowing town of Bermatingen (featuring historic half-timbered houses and the Catholic parish church of St. Georg (14th cen., renovated in the 18th cen.)) is situated just 2.5 km west of Markdorf. Hagnau (pop. 1400) is just a 3 km walk or bicycle ride down the lakeshore path or the high path from Meersburg. Its really just a "stone's throw" if you take the regularly scheduled ship or drive via the B 31. From the parking lot at the entrance to town, follow Kapellenstrasse directly down to the landing on the lake shore. Winegrowing and fishing have set the tone of economic life in the pastoral village on the northern shore of the lake for centuries: today, fruit-growing and tourism have joined those traditional economic factors. From Kapellenstrasse, Seestrasse leads off to the east, also marked by the romantic "Malerhäusle" with its half-timbered structure. The Irseer Hof (the mighty stone structure with the hipped roof) and the prince-bishop's Zehnthaus (to the right) clearly show the importance the ecclesiastical rulers attached to the fertile region. Past the tourist information office, we cross the next street and

View over Hagnau with the Catholic parish church over to the Swiss shoreline with the snow-covered summits of the Alps.

Tourist Office, Seestrasse 16, D-88709 Hagnau,
Phone: 07532/430021, Fax: 430020
The Little Museum: *April through end-October, Sunday - Thursday 10:00 AM - 12:00 noon, 2:00 - 5:00 PM, and by appointment.*

proceed about 100 m where the former Weingartner Hof comes into view. Its gateway spans the narrow street. Today, it is the home of the city hall and Winegrowers' Association, among other things. We continue along the lakeshore for the time being and turn left before the miniature golf course. There is an interesting winepress beneath a roof here: it is an original "Baumtorkel" (1747). There are only about ten of its kind in Germany. It functions by means of a spindle according to the principle of a one-armed lever. Five labourers had to work here for 8 hours in order to press out up to 5 tonnes of grapes. It is the last press of its kind in the winegrowing village of Hagnau, which at one time had 30 of these to transform the year's ripe fruit into exquisite wine.

Hagnau: statue of Pastor Hansjakob in front of the city hall facade.

Now we cross over the courtyard of the city hall to the left and then cross Strandbadstrasse. After about 50 m, we come to a Hagnau landmark, the late Gothic parish church of St. John the Baptist. The remarkable 48 m spire dates back in part to the Romanesque period, while its nave and choir were renovated in Baroque style in 1729. It still has two exquisitely carved figures from the 15th century, though. The most famous figure, however, has been in the Swiss church of Münsterlingen Cloister since February of 1963. In keeping with a centuries-old tradition, the bust of John the Evangelist (16th cent.) is carried over the lake between Hagnau and Münsterlingen in a solemn procession each time the "See-gfrörne" comes - i.e. when the lake freezes over entirely. It does not switch its location again until the next reoccurrence of the "Seegfrörne", which, as experience has shown, can take many years.

Heinrich Hansjakob was pastor of this church from 1869-1884: he made a name for himself as a writer and active politician, among other things. He founded the first Winegrowers' Cooperative of Baden in Hagnau in 1881, thereby helping the local winegrowers to get fair prices for their improved varieties of grapes. The Salmannsweiler Hof, a magnificent half-timbered structure with a staggered gable and partial hip roof, is in back of the Catholic church in the midst of vineyards. Back on Kirchweg, we follow it along to the right to another historic half-timbered house, the hotel, restaurant and café "Zum Löwen", a huge building with a double hip roof. The next street to the right, Winzerstrasse, takes us to the last of the official monastic houses in Hagnau, the extensive three-wing complex of the Schussenrieder Hof.

On our way back towards the parking lot - on Hauptstrasse here - and/or back to the landing, we pass by the fully automated hotel information system in front of Hagnauer Hof. It can provide you with information on hotel vacancies in town. For active vacationers, the village offers a surprising variety of possibilities for swimming (on the natural sand beach) and fishing, sailing and surfing, for tennis and miniature golf, for bicycle-riding and hiking (40 km marked trails, as well as instructional trails about fruit- and winegrowing). For those who are less athletically inclined, we can also recommend a visit to the "Kleines Museum" (doll rooms and toys), a ride in a horse-drawn carriage or a boat ride on Lake Constance.

Immenstaad

The peaceful resort town of Immenstaad (population 5900) is situated 4 km east of Hagnau. On the way there, just outside of Hagnau, it is worth taking a side-trip to the Frenkenbach part of Immenstaad and its Romanesque fortified Church of St. Oswald (ca. 1200), one of the oldest churches in the entire Linzgau region.

The first of Immenstaad's three palaces lies halfway between Hagnau and Immenstaad: Kirchberg Palace, constructed in the 18th century as a summer residence of the Cistercian Abbey at Salem. In 1802, it passed into the possession of the Margrave of Baden. A street opposite the palace leads to another part of Immenstaad

Immenstaad: Kirchberg Palace, built in the 18th century as a summer residence for the Cistercian Abbey of Salem.

Tourist Office, Postfach 1109, D-88090 Immenstaad, Phone: 07545/201-110, Fax: 201-208
Museum of Local History at the "Montfort" House: April - September, Saturday, Sunday, holidays 2:00 - 6:00 PM.
Café Museum "Zum Puppenhaus": April - September, 11:00 AM - 6:00 PM, March and October 2:00 - 6:00 PM, closed Mondays.

Immenstaad: half-timbered building "Schwörerhaus" (1578); in the background, the late Gothic parish church of St. Jodokus.

called Kippenhausen. Its late Gothic Kirche Mariä Himmelfahrt (i.e. " Church of the Ascension of Mary") was renovated in Baroque style in the 18th century. In town, you can visit two museums and a gallery in the magnificently renovated "Montfort" House. To the right, the Hohberg rises almost 60 m above the level of Lake Constance between Kippenhausen and Hersberg Palace, providing a fine view.

Passing well-tended orchards, vineyards, meadows and, finally, Hersberg Palace, we reach the centre of Immenstaad, marked by the parish church of St. Jodokus. What makes this late Gothic house of worship especially appealing is its striking tower, which gives the impression of being well-fortified. Opposite the parish church to the south is St. Michael's Chapel (built in 1713), which comes from the Baroque period, to the east a typically Alemannic stilted half-timbered structure, the Schwörerhaus, built in 1578.

Bachstrasse leads down to the landing, which also has an adjacent yachting har-

bour. The town has a second yachting harbour including camping grounds at the aforementioned Kirchberg Palace, and a third one, also combined with camping grounds, at Helmsdorf Palace, about 1 km east of the centre of town. There is a tennis court and a beach swimming area next to the former palace. Inside the palace, visitors can dine in an elegant atmosphere and try the home-brewed beer.

The town offers a varied recreational programme for the whole family in other aspects as well, ranging from excursions into the marvellous countryside to tennis, table tennis or water sports. The beach swimming area and the indoor pool, open all year round, guarantee that the fun will go on in any weather.

What better place could there be to relax from a busy day of sightseeing over a cup of coffee or dinner than in one of the numerous restaurants and cafés. They also offer the appropriate setting to bid farewell to an impressive resort town that attracts many tourists and vacationers.

21

Friedrichshafen

It is 10 km from Immenstaad to Friedrichshafen on the B 31, but we already reach Fischbach, which is part of Friedrichsha-fen, just 2 km past Helmsdorf Palace and - after our stay in Baden - the first town in Württemberg. In a country setting among orchards and meadows, it is mainly popular in the summer-

An aerial view of Friedrichshafen: on the shore above the large boat harbour is the modern Graf-Zeppelin-Haus, the towers of the palace church are visible on the peninsula.

Tourist Information, Postfach 2460, D-88014 Friedrichshafen, Phone: 07541/3001-0, Fax: 72588
Zeppelin Museum "Technology and Art": *May-Oct. Tuesday-Sunday 10:00 AM - 6:00 PM, Nov.-April Tuesday-Sunday 10:00 AM-5:00 PM.* **School Museum:** *April-Oct. daily 10:00 AM-5:00 PM, Nov.-March daily except Mondays from 2:00-5:00 PM,* **Palace Church:** *mid-April - Sept. 9:00 AM - 6:00 PM, Oct. 9:00 AM - 5:00 PM.*

time due to its outdoor pool and lake swimming area with a natural beach.

Two km down the road, we reach **Manzell,** an industrial suburb of Friedrichsha-fen. Count Ferdinand von Zeppelin once assembled the first dirigible airship, the 128 m long "LZ 1", in a floating hall here. It went aloft for the first time on July 2, 1900. In 1909, Zeppelin moved to Fried-richshafen, but just a short time later, Claudius Dornier founded his aeroplane factory in Manzell (in 1914). His factory primarily specialised in flying boats and amphibious planes. After a ten year lull at the end of World War II, the factory took up production of aeroplanes again in 1955 and is still producing today, although it is now part of Daimler Benz-AG.

Another 5 km down the road, we reach the heart of the regional administrative centre of **Friedrichshafen,** which is, after Constance, the second largest city on Lake Constance (population 55,000). It gets its name from the first Württemberg King Friedrich I, who united the old city of Buchhorn (9th cent., city charter in 1215, free imperial city from 1275-1802) with the village of Hofen and had the harbour built. The construction of dirigibles has made Friedrichshafen famous. Announced takeoffs and landings drew huge crowds of spectators. In the First World War, airships were used to bombard Paris and London. As majestic as they were, however, the "flying cigars" were also easy prey for more maneuverable enemy fighters . People realised already back in 1917 that Zeppelins could not keep up with the pace at which modern aviation was developing. The Zeppelin works had already begun production of military aeroplanes in 1912, however, thereby adjusting to the changing times.

Friedrichshafen: a historic photograph of airship LZ 127, the "Graf Zeppelin", which circumnavigated the globe in 1929.

Despite this, small series of airships were still built, such as the "LZ 127", which circumnavigated the globe in 1929, and the "LZ 129" - 245 m in length, 41 m in diameter. Another dirigible belonging to this class was the "Hindenburg", which exploded and burned at the mooring mast in Lakehurst, New Jersey (USA) on May 6, 1937, on its 11th flight to North America, thereby marking the end of the age of airships.

Friedrichshafen's **Zeppelin Museum,** encompassing approx. 4000 m2 in the former access to a 33 m reconstruction of the passenger and crew quarters of the "LZ 129 - Hindenburg" mentioned above, definitely a unique attraction in our fast-paced world. A zeppelin started flying over Friedrichshafen and Lake Constance again in 1997. It is "Zeppelin of New Technologies," called LZ N07 for short. The craft, which measures 69 m long and has a diameter of 14 m, can carry two pilots and twelve passengers in its snow-white cabin. The museum also has a supplementary exhib-

The Zeppelin NT marks the start of a new era in airship aviation.

▲ *Writing parlour of LZ 129.*

▲ *Zeppelin Museum: art exhibit.*

harbour station at the ship and ferry harbour, was opened in 1996. This is the world's largest collection on the history of dirigibles, documenting their development and the life of Count Zeppelin in pictures and models. Via a gangway, visitors have it on the art of the Lake Constance region from the late Middle Ages on.

Starting in 1943, Friedrichshafen suffered the same fate as many industrial German cities: massive air-raids accompanied by extensive destruction of historic buildings and structures. Therefore, the number of sights to see in Friedrichshafen is mainly limited to the area around the lakeshore such as the area here in front of the harbour station. Aside from the passenger ships for excursions, the important car ferries to and from Romanshorn (Switzerland) arrive at and depart from this point, also an attraction for motorised visitors.

We now follow Seestrasse and then Uferstrasse - with a terrific view of the lake - along to the west. A monument in the city gardens at the level of the yachting harbour serves as a reminder of Friedrichshafen's most famous son as does the following post-modern Count Zeppelin House. It was built as a modern cultural and conference centre with rooms for 5 to 1500 persons. There is a restaurant with a café overlooking the lake and, adjacent to it, a pub with skittle alleys.

We now leave the lakeshore promenade - one of the longest and most beautiful anywhere on Lake Constance - and take Olgastrasse to get to Friedrichstrasse, which we follow along a short distance to the left. We soon encounter the Schulmuseum (i.e. "School Museum"), where visitors can marvel at three originally furnished classrooms from the years 1850, 1900 and 1930. In another 16 rooms, you can see artefacts of the development of schools since the time of the monastery and convent schools - including the punishments, teaching and learning materials, and teachers' working conditions.

Just a few meters back in the direction we came from on Friedrichsstrasse and Olgastrasse, we follow along Klosterstrasse which forks off to the right. In expansive park grounds, we can already recognise from a distance the 55 m high "onion towers" of the **Schlosskirche,** which are the trademark of the city. Built 1695-1701 under the direction of architect Christian Thumb, it is regarded as the loveliest Baroque church in upper Swabia. It has served as a Protestant church since 1812 - with the exception of the years 1944-51, when it was closed due to war damage and renovation work. The ornate

Friedrichshafen: the Baroque onion towers of the Palace Church (1695-1701) are the trademark of the city and an attraction worth seeing.

Friedrichshafen: Nave and choir of the Baroque palace church.

stucco work (representative of the Wessobrunner School) makes it worth a look inside. Up until 1802, the church belonged to Hofen Abbey, the buildings were erected in 1654 on commission from the Benedictines in Weingarten. After secularisation in 1802, the complex became state property, was renovated and served as a summer residence for the Württemberg kings between 1824 and 1918. Today, it is the residence of Friedrich, Duke of Württemberg. Therefore, the palace and park are closed to the public.

Friedrichshafen's beach swimming area is situated in the extension of Klosterstrasse: there are indoor pools on Ehlerstrasse and in the Ailingen part of the city.

The advantage that a relatively large tour-

A view of Lake Constance across the palace park. The coat of arms of the owners, the Dukes of Württemberg, adorns the gate.

ist city such as Friedrichshafen has over smaller competitors is, undoubtedly, the larger range of recreational activities available. Aside from numerous possibilities for water sports (fishing, swimming, boating, sailing, and windsurfing), there are also opportunities for billiards, skittles, miniature golf, tennis, bicycle-riding, and horse-riding as well as more exotic activities such as badminton and squash, discos and saunas, go-cart, balloon-rides and sightseeing flights. In fact, Friedrichshafen has its own airport, in the north-eastern district of Löwental, with scheduled flights to Stuttgart, Frankfurt, Berlin, Zurich, and Geneva. The industrial estate (incl. the Zeppelin metal works) and the expansive **Trade Fair Grounds,** where the International Lake Constance Trade Fair (consumer and investment goods) is held annually in the spring and the even more well-known "Interboot" (water sports) in the fall, are located to the north of downtown.

The northern district of **Ailingen** (4 km) is also worth a visit. It is the holiday resort known as the "Orchard on Lake Constance". It offers inexpensive family holidays in private homes and farm houses as well as cosy hotels and country inns. This district was the national winner of the "Family Holidays in Germany" contest in 1990. Aside from a variety of garden and summer festivals, Ailingen also specialises in offering events for children such as horse-rides, rides in horse-drawn carriages and pony-treks, and bicycle and hiking tours on a well-maintained network of paths. Its main attraction, however, is the fun and adventure pool specially designed for children - with a heated outdoor wave pool - one of a kind in the Lake Constance region.

After continuing along 6 km in the direction of Lindau, we reach **Eriskirch.** This village at the mouth of the Schussen is especially noted for its lakeshore strip with wild orchards and the offshore reeds separating it from Lake Constance proper. The Eriskircher Ried (i.e. "Eriskirch Marsh", 550 ha) has been a nature conservation area since 1938 and serves as a home for rare plants and a reserve and resting place for many bird species. Nature lovers can become more acquainted with the marsh under the direction of a knowledgeable guide.

Most of all in Eriskirch, the Gothic parish and pilgrimage church of "Unserer Lieben Frau" ("Church of Our Lady") is worth a visit. The present-day house of God was built around 1400. Although it was renovated in Baroque style after fire damage from the Thirty Years' War, fortunately, the frescoes from the time immediately following original construction were retained as was the miracle working image "Unserer Lieben Frau von Eriskirch" ("Our Lady of Eriskirch", 14th cent., above the left side alter) and two choir window glassworks which commemorate the founder of the church, Heinrich von Montfort (15th cent.). A picturesque, covered wooden bridge (from 1828) resting on 96 posts spans the Schussen close to the church. Although Eriskirch is not directly on Lake Constance, it still has a swimming area on the lake to offer its guests, along with a parking lot for hikers, bicycles for hire, and the opportunity to spend a "holiday down on the farm".

Eriskirch: choir window (15th cen.) in the parish church.

Langenargen

The municipality of Langenargen (pop. 7000) is situated 4 km past Eriskirch, about the same distance from Mariabrunn as well, and off the national highway, on the flat shore of Lake Constance. There is a large woodland, which is replaced by fruit groves towards the lake, north of the Bierkeller-Waldeck section of town. To the west is the mouth of the Schussen in Lake Constance - this is where the Eriskircher Ried begins -, to the east is the Argen, which gave the town its name. There is also a nature preserve at the mouth of this river, even though the river itself is forced into a narrow bed. This municipality is actively committed to nurturing and preserving natural and cultural landscapes in other ways too, such as wild orchards and intact biotopes.

Langenargen's trademark is the exotic-looking Montfort Palace, located on a pen-

A view of the wildlife preservation area between Eriskirch and Langenargen and out over Lake Constance to the Swiss shore.

Culture and Tourist Office, Obere Seestrasse 1, D-88085 Langenargen, Phone: 07543/9330-92, Fax: 4696
Montfort Palace: *April and Oct. daily 10:00 AM - 12:00 noon and 1:00 PM - 4:00 PM.* **Langenargen Museum:** *April - mid. Oct. daily except Mondays from 10:00 AM - 12:00 noon and 2:00 - 5:00 PM.*

Langenargen: night-time romanticism around Montfort Palace, built after 1787 in "Moresque style".

insula before the centre of town. It gets its name from the lineage of the Counts von Montfort. Their traditional palace was in Götzis (Vorarlberg); however, several lines split off in the 13th century. Around 1300, the counts gained possession of Langenargen, where they dwelled in Argen Castle until the 18th century. Their line died out in 1787 and the castle went to ruins. The new family of owners, the royal house of Württemberg, had the present-day palace constructed in its place, similar to the Wilhelma in Stuttgart in "Moresque style". Therefore, no member of the family the palace is named after ever lived in Montfort Palace. Today, it serves as a concert and exhibition building with large and small halls and a terrace café. This is where the Langenargen Summer Concerts are held, featuring artists from all over the world. Dance and theatre evenings are other popular events. Classy musical entertainment can also be heard at the concert shell in the palace park, which also presents an opportunity to play an entertaining game of garden chess, miniature golf or boccie. Opposite the palace is the Kavalierhaus with a gallery and the Kulturcafé ("Culture Café").

The Baroque parish church of St. Martin rises on the edge of the palace park. Construction on it was started in 1718 by or-

Langenargen: Montfort Palace, landmark of the resort town on Lake Constance.

der of Count Anton III von Montfort. It contains lovely ceiling frescoes from Anton Maulbertsch. The broad Marktplatz with the city hall, museum and Münzhof (now a cultural centre with city library) is behind the church. The museum is in the former parish rectory (18th cent.) and offers artwork from the history of the town. Among other things, it has on display a piece from the artist Franz Anton Maulbertsch, (son of the aforementioned Anton Maulbertsch), who was born in Langenargen. He left the town at the early age of 16, built a career for himself in Vienna and developed into the most significant German Baroque painter of the 18th century. Aside from his painting "Schlüsselübergabe an Petrus" (i.e. "Passing of the Key to Peter"), the exhibition includes some portraits from Andreas Brugger as well as works by artists who frequently spent their summers working here.

If you walk along the Untere Seestrasse to the north-west, you will pass the Staatliche Institut für Seenforschung und Seenbewirtschaftung (i.e. "State Institute for Lake Research and Cultivation"), then, fur-ther out of town, the beach swimming area and, finally, the surfing area, before arriving at the Schussen. There is a second hiking and bicycle trail leading to the sport centre with tennis courts and a tennis hall in the town district of Bierkeller-Waldeck. To the east of the tourist office at the ships landing, there is a protected gondola harbour and sailing school. Behind those, you can find the public park of Uhlandplatz, which extends almost all the way to Mühlgraben. Remaining on the lakeshore, we reach the surfing club, an outdoor swimming area and, finally, the sailing school and a fish hatchery.

From this point, there is a highway leading north in the direction of Lindau. Parallel to that, you can view the oldest cable suspension bridge in Germany (from

Langenargen: rosary picture, in the parish church of St. Martin, depicting the birth of Christ.

Langenargen: colourful Baroque altars in the parish church.

1898) spanning the Argen. Its cousins in the USA, the Golden Gate Bridge and the Brooklyn Bridge, are much more famous. Langenargen likes to call itself "the sun porch on Lake Constance", since the town faces the midday sun. Although it has relatively few spectacular, historic structures, it is still a pleasing place to visit thanks to its location on the lake, framed by fruit-tree meadows and fields of hops, not to mention the peaceful atmosphere far off the heavily travelled national highway. The great variety of recreational activities and the attractive shopping possibilities, in the arcade as well, make Langenargen a beloved resort town.

Langenargen: the cable suspension bridge over the Argen, Germany's oldest.

Kressbronn Nonnenhorn

6

Kressbronn

Halfway between Friedrichshafen and Lindau lies the town of Kressbronn (population 7000) direct on Lake Constance, surrounded by large fruit plantations. A special attraction for numerous vacationers is the cherry- and apple-blossom time, an unforgettable natural spectacle. The Kressbronn Blossom Festival and the instructional trails for fruit- and winegrowing, which has been set up at the northern edge of town with a fantastic view, are indicative of the extent to which the town is tied to this form of agriculture. Of course, Kressbronn also offers its vacationers the lake with the gamut of water sports opportunities, including a natural sand beach, guided hikes and bicycle tours (80 km of marked trails) and covered wagon rides. When the weather is less favourable, there is still an indoor swimming pool, the sauna, and the "Haus des Gastes" (Guest Centre).

The "Lände" House in the Schlösslepark near the landing is the home of the Guest Centre, where many different events are held. The Tourist Information Office is located in the "Schlössle", which is also where you can find the indoor pool, water-treading facilities, and a bandstand.

Kressbronn: view of the idyllic resort town and Lake Constance over to the summits of the Swiss Alps with the Säntis Massif.

Information

Kressbronn Tourist Office in the Schlössle, Seestrasse 20, D-88079 Kressbronn, Phone: 07543/9665-0, Fax: 9665-15
Nonnenhorn Tourist Office, Seehalde 2, D-88149 Nonnenhorn, Phone: 08382/8250, Fax: 890-76

The centre of town is situated beyond the train tracks. This is where the city hall (18th cent.), the Catholic parish church and the Baroque Eligiuskapelle ("Eligius Chapel", 18th cent.) are located. The latter of these serves as a memorial to the dead of both world wars.

Nonnenhorn

Although Kressbronn is still part of Württemberg, Nonnenhorn (pop. 1600) is located in the narrow section of Lake Constance belonging to Bavaria. Much has been done in the peaceful village to ensure that guests have the most pleasant stay possible. For instance, the municipality has set up a beach swimming area, a heated swimming pool and a warming hall including a solarium, to ensure that swimming is possible even if it is not the middle of summer outside. Aside from that, there is a bicycle and boat rental, a library with a readers' corner and facilities for tennis, miniature golf, outdoor chess, and skittle.

In the extension of the landing dock, you can find the tourist office in Haus Stedi. Seestrasse leads us to the left (from the landing dock) to Kapellenplatz with the early Gothic chapel of St. Jakobus the Elder (15th cent.). A large erratic block by the chapel was transformed into the "Seegefrörnenstein" ("Seegefrörnen Stone") without further ado - with the dates when Lake Constance has frozen over. Heading east, you come to the oldest and largest remaining winepress in the Lake Constance region. It was in use from 1591 to 1950 and documents the fondness of the winegrowing village of Nonnenhorn for the (liquid) fruit of the vine, which guests can still taste in refined restaurants - accompanied by fish specialities from Lake Constance and fresh fruit, which thrives everywhere around Nonnenhorn.

Aerial view of the south-eastern shoreline of Lake Constance: Nonnenhorn is in the foreground, Wasserburg on the narrow peninsula; Lindau is further back. Bregenz Forest is in the distant background.

Wasserburg

Separated from Nonnenhorn by a bay, the peninsula with the Wasserburg juts out far into the lake. Bicycle and hiking trails close to the shore connect both towns with one another and provide an unobstructed view of the romantic ensemble of historic structures with the striking onion tower of the parish church and the tall edifice of the palace - especially from the vantage point known as the Maler-winkel ("Painter's Corner"). There is a large wildlife preservation area between the trail and the shore at the point where Nonnenhorn Bay cuts the widest swath. Just behind the miniature golf course, the "Fuggersäule", a column adorned with reliefs (1720), marks the place where the moat between the mainland and the island was filled in at the behest of then Fugger family of merchants, who were

Wasserburg: the constellation of peninsula and parish church, rectory and harbour is a Wasserburg landmark.

Wasserburg Tourist Office, D-88142 Wasserburg,
Phone: 08382/887474, Fax: 89042
Malhaus Museum: *May to October daily except Mondays from 10:00 AM - 12:00 noon, Wednesday and Saturday also open 3:00 - 5:00 PM.*

the owners of the palace at that time. That way, they were able to avoid having to renovate the old drawbridge, thereby creating the present-day peninsula. The tall building on Nonnenhorn Bay is the palace which was in the possession of the Fuggers from 1592 until well into the 18th century. They established a mint. The palace was built in the 14th century on the foundation of the old castle (8th cent., destroyed in 1358) and came into the possession of the mighty Counts von Montfort as a gift from the Abbey of St. Gall in 1537. Wasserburg itself (present pop. 3000), first appears in documents in 784 and is one of the oldest settlements in the Lake Constance region. Today, the palace is home to a renowned hotel which has a fabulous terrace facing Lake Constance.

The Malhaus (1596) is situated opposite the hotel: it presently houses a museum of local history. It holds testimonials from the history of Wasserburg for our generation and those to come; documents from areas of life that were vital for the town, such as fishing, shipping, agriculture, fruit- and winegrowing as well as objects of interpretative art. The main structure of the parish church of St. Georg is - just like that of the palace - very old, even though there are hardly any remnants of the previous churches (proof of their existence dates back to 784). The present-day structure was put up in 1595, after a fire destroyed the old church. The cemetery at the tip of the peninsula is even older. Its tin-covered wall has withstood the waves of Lake Constance for centuries. Visitors have a nice view of the lake over the wall. The cemetery and church are the reason that Wasserburg is also a stopping point on the "Upper Swabian Baroque Road". The church tower contains the tombstone of Bartholomäus Heuchlinger. He was the head bailiff of the Fuggers and one of the main antagonists behind the cruel witch trials of the 17th century in Wasserburg.

The "Haus des Gastes" is also located on the peninsula. It has a reading room,
rooms for watching television, playing and for special events, including a restaurant and a café with a large garden terrace directly on the lake. Wasserburg has a great deal to offer its guests outside of these rooms, too: aside from all kinds of water sports, particularly the recreation, sport and leisure centre in the east of the peninsula with a heated swimming pool, warming hall, swimming channel, large lawn, sauna, massages, solarium, windsurfing school, and cosy restaurants, as well as a boat rental, a sailing school, and a tennis and squash hall. There is a monument to "Lieber Augustin" (i.e. "Dear Augustin") by the parking lot of the leisure centre on the lakeshore. It is dedicated to author Horst Wolfram Geißler, who published the amiable novel "Der liebe Augustin" in 1921 and whose final resting place is in Wasserburg Cemetery. Of course, Wasserburg is also an ideal starting point for excursions by ship or bus, thanks to its location on the east part of the Obersee or "Upper Lake" (Allgäu, Austria, Liechtenstein, Switzerland). However, the hinterland is also worth paying a visit to: there are numerous bicycle and hiking trails leading to the town districts of Reutenen (peaceful location directly on the lake), Hege, Hattnau, Selmnau, Hengnau, Bettnau, and Bodolz (serene "holiday on the farm"). Along the way, we pass through fruit plantations, woods, meadows, and fields, before finally arriving at such beauteous outlooks as St. Antonius Mountain with its chapel of the same name (via Selmnau), Martinshöhe (via Hengnau) or the landscape conservation area around the Bichelweiher. If you are looking for home-style, inexpensive restaurants, you are sure to find the right thing in the town districts listed above, or you can dine in the main town of Wasserburg where the restaurants offer many local specialities from the kitchen and cellar. If you prefer rustic fare, you can find a proper rustic snack anywhere, rounded off with an "Obstler" (i.e. "fruit brandy"), the typical digestive in the Lake Constance region.

Wasserburg:
a view across the peninsula with the parish church and Lake Constance towards the

Austrian Rhine Valley. The peaks of the Vorarlberg Alps are visible in the background.

Lindau

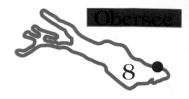

Three kilometres east of Wasserburg is **Bad Schachen,** the best-known part of Lindau. It advanced to the rank of a spa due to its iron and sulphur springs. Magnificent old villas, such as the modern Hotel Schachen-Schlössle in the town centre or the Hotel Bad Schachen adjacent to the lake, the oldest parts of which were built in 1752, are tucked away in sprawling parks. Nearly 100 years later, a wealthy merchant had the Classical Villa Lindenhof built in a huge park. Today the building houses the Lindau Peace Museum.

Lindau seen from the air: above the green Gartenstadt is the old city centre on the island.

Lindau Tourist Office, Postfach 1325, D-88103 Lindau, phone 08382/260030, fax 260026
Haus zum Cavazzen and City Museum:
Tuesday - Sunday 10:00 - 12:00 AM - noon and 2:00 - 5:00 PM, guided tours by appointment.

Fall idyll: a view from Bad Schachen to Lindau.

If you want to get to know Lindau better, it is advisable to find a parking spot without a time limit (P1, P3 or P5 - on the island). There is a free shuttle bus to the island from the first two parking lots mentioned, which are on the mainland. Before starting our tour at the lakeside harbour, let us briefly consider the history of the city. A convent was founded on the island in 800 AD. Lindau is first mentioned in the annals in 882. After the locality was granted the status of an imperial city, it soon numbered among the wealthiest settlements in Swabia and received the honorary title of the "Venice of Swabia". Long-distance trading with Italy remained the basis of its prosperity even in the following centuries. There was a weekly link to Milan from the 15th to the 19th century, via which letters, goods, and travellers could be transported safely over the Alps with horse-drawn vehicles or pack animals. The town is still proud of the Imperial Diet of 1496, which was held within its walls.

As was also the case with many other trading towns, the shifting of trading routes toward seaports brought an end to economic prosperity. In 1802, the city lost its immediacy; it was annexed to the Kingdom of Bavaria three years later. But the city knew how to make a virtue of necessity and mar-

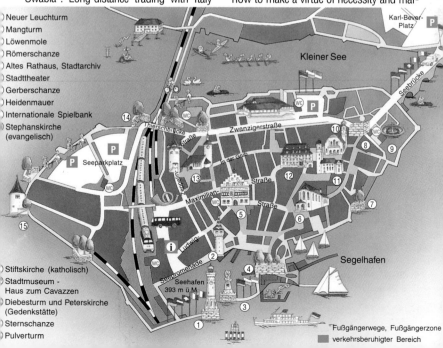

) Neuer Leuchtturm
) Mangturm
) Löwenmole
) Römerschanze
) Altes Rathaus, Stadtarchiv
) Stadttheater
) Gerberschanze
) Heidenmauer
) Internationale Spielbank
) Stephanskirche (evangelisch)

) Stiftskirche (katholisch)
) Stadtmuseum - Haus zum Cavazzen
) Diebesturm und Peterskirche (Gedenkstätte)
) Sternschanze
) Pulverturm

Lindau:
The New Lighthouse and the Bavarian lion guard the entrance to the harbour.

Lindau: The Lakeside Promenade above the berths of the sport boats. In the middle is the Old Lighthouse, which, as the "Mangturm", was part of the city's fortifications in Medieval times.

ket its historical buildings. The tourist trade already began to develop with the advent of the steamships (1835) and connection to the railway network (1853). Today, all of the buildings on the island are protected cultural monuments. Every year, the city registers 200,000 overnight guest stays in the city and around one million day guests.

Our tour of the island begins at Lindau's most photographed spot: the harbour. At the end of its western breakwater stands the 33 m high **New Lighthouse** (built 1856). From its observation platform, one has a magnificent view over the island all the way to Gartenstadt on the mainland, but also across the lake to Bregenz and the massive Alpine panorama. Its counterpart on the east side is a 6 m high **Bavarian lion,** which has also watched over the harbour since it was expanded in the

mid-19th century. These, together with the **Old Lighthouse** on the land side of the harbour basin, are the hallmarks of Lindau. The tower, which can also be climbed, belonged to the city's Medieval defences since the 13th century, when it was known as the "Mangturm". Its colourfully glazed roofing tiles dominate the lakeshore promenade. It adjoins the central railway station, which has a ticket window where tickets for ships are also available. The Tourist Information Centre and the bus station are right nearby. The rest of the lakeside promenade is lined with inviting restaurant terraces. The Römerschanze on the east side of the harbour was once a separate island. Like many other little islands, it was joined to the main island by backfilling the space in-between. Today, its lakeshore is home to a shipyard harbour and

The Lindavia Fountain in front of historic Old Town Hall.

Lindau: The "Wall of the Heathens" and St. Stephen's Tower.

sailing school, the sailing harbour, and the Römerbad, one of the city's five lake baths. On the way back from the Römerschanze, we turn left one block after the harbour basin into the Brettermarkt and then right into the Reichsplatz with the monumental Lindavia Fountain made of red marble (late 19th cen.). In the background are the colourfully painted, staggered gables of the Old Town Hall. It was built 1422-36 - in what was then still a vineyard - and modified repeatedly. The Verkündererker (Crier's Window), which is reached via covered stairs, and the large Gothic hall in which the 1496 Imperial Diet was held have been preserved. Today the ground floor holds the one-time imperial city's extensive library: 23000 books and manuscripts from the 14th century on. The City Archives and a reading room are also housed in this historic building.

At its eastern end, Ludwigstraße spreads out to become Barfüßerplatz (literally, "Square of the Barefoot Ones"), named for the Franciscan Monastery (13th cen.) and its friars (who were known as Barfüßer in reference to their asceticism). The city has kept its theatre and a concert hall in the one-time Bar-

füßerkirche (Franciscan Church) since 1951. At the end of the romantic Fischergasse ("Fishermen's Alley") is a defensive tower preserved from the city fortifications of the Staufer era, the so-called "Heidenmauer" ("Wall of the Heathens"). This is where the city gardens begin, the grounds of which are home to the Bayerische Spielbank ("Bavarian Casino"). The gardens are transsected by the street that, via the lake bridge, represents the only connection to the mainland for road vehicles. Besides the lake bridge, there is only a dike for the railway connection, which can also be crossed by pedestrians and bicyclists. The body of water between the two links to the mainland is called the "Kleiner See" ("Little Lake") and is especially popular with boaters as a relatively risk-free area. Right next to the Little Lake is the modern Inselhalle Complex with harmoniously designed, modernly conceived rooms. It helps to secure Lindau's reputation as an attractive city for conventions and trade fairs. The Schmiedgasse brings us to the Marktplatz (Market Square), where the Protestant Stephanskirche ("St. Stephen's Church", built 1180, Baroque modification 1782) and the Catholic Stiftskirche ("Collegiate

Lindau: The richly decorated facade of the building "Zum Cavazzen", which today houses the City Museum.

Church") stand side by side harmoniously. The Stiftskirche has stood since 1752 on the site of the Romanesque Abbey, which belonged to the once powerful Princely Convent and was destroyed by the Great Fire of 1728.

On the west side of marketplace stands one of the loveliest patrician houses on Lake Constance, the "Haus zum Cavazzen". It was erected right after the Great Fire by the Appenzell-based master builder Grubenmann. The building houses the City Museum and exhibits an extensive collection of furnish-

The Cramergasse leads us in a curve to the broad, central Maximilianstraße, which was once the street where the patricians, merchants, and chief wardens of the guilds lived. Today it is part of the city's pedestrian mall, lined by many stately Gothic and Renaissance facades. The historical buildings bear names such as "Sünfzen" (sünfzen = slurping, inn, meeting place of the rich merchants until the 19th cen.), "Regenbogen" ("rainbow"), "Schnegg" ("snail"), "Pflug" ("plow"), "Brotlaube" ("oergola")

◀ *Lindau: Historic 14th cen. facades in Maximilianstraße.*

▼ *Maximilianstraße: Inn "Zum Sünfzen".*

ings and art objects from patrician cultural circles as well as mechanical musical instruments. Among the paintings, the portrait of Friederike von Bretzenheim is especially impressive. She was the illegitimate daughter of Elector Karl Theodor von Pfalz-Bayern and a Mannheim actress; until 1802, she was the last Mother Abbess of the aforementioned convent. The author Horst Wolfram Geißler was so impressed by this portrait, that he made her a character in one of his novels, the subject of the passionate admiration of a common man, the music-box maker and title hero of the book "Der Liebe Augustin" ("Dear Augustine"). The sprawling building at the marketplace is called "Zum Baumgarten" (built sometime after 1728).

and "Rad" ("wheel"). Typical of these houses are the staggered gables, narrow bay windows, massive dormer windows, and "Brotlauben" (ground floor access galleries or pergolas). Fountains, inviting street cafes and a virtually endless, colourful row of shops and boutiques are all part of the streetscape today, which looks like the set for a historical movie.

Via the Schafgasse, to the right, we soon come to the Peterskirche ("St. Peter's Church"). The church is some 1000 years old, making one of the oldest surviving works of architecture in the Lake Constance region. Although transformed into a Veteran's Memorial Chapel in 1928, it is worth seeing for the paintings on the inside alone: they are

*Maximilianstraße: A view of the tow-
ers of St. Stephen's Church (left) and
the Collegiate Church.*

the only surviving frescoes of the famous
painter Hans Holbein the Elder (ca. 1480).
In the immediate vicinity of the Peterskirche, the Diebsturm ("Thieve's Tower")
(1380), also known as the Malefizturm
("Malfeasance Tower"), is a reminder of
the times when cities were ringed with
walls. H.W. Geißler wrote parts of his popular novel "Der liebe Augustin" in the nearby inn "Goldenes Lamm" (Paradiesplatz).
On our way down Paradiesplatz towards
the railway dike we now encounter remnants
of the city's fortifications everywhere: the
Alte Zeughaus (Old Armoury), the earth-
works known as the Lindenschanze and,

Lindau: Tower of St. Peter's Church

on the other side of the railway bridge, the Sternschanze. On the mainland opposite is the Aeschacher Bad, one of Lindau's bathing beaches. Those for whom the water temperature in Lake Constance is too cold might want to try the City Indoor Pool, Eichwald Bathing Beach (3 heated outdoor pools, 78 m water slide - both in the Reutin section of Lindau) or the heated pool at Lindau-Oberreitnau Recreation Centre.

An elegant promenade leads along the shore and offers a magnificent view of the lake. The city filled in the grounds around the parking lot in 1968-69 and thus increased the area of the island from 62 to 68 ha. The pointy-turreted Pulverturm (Powder Tower, 1508, once known as the "Grüner Turm" or "Green Tower"), which stands on part of the original area of the island, looks very romantic. Finally,

the lakeshore promenade leads us to the harbour, which is where our tour began. Of course, a city like Lindau has a lot to offer in the way of leisure time activities. Besides the swimming facilities already mentioned, there are possibilities for virtually all water sports, golf courses and tennis courts, hiking and bicycling; in City Park, the Casino awaits you with roulette and black jack. The Tourist Information Centre offers guided tours of the city for grown-ups and children. A wheelchair-accessible path around the island, with suitable toilets and telephone booths, shows that the city also has a heart for the physically challenged.

Cultural events are also considered to be the mark of a modern community. In Lindau, it is not only traditional artistic pursuits such as theatre, folklore and clas-

Lindau: the Medieval Powder Tower.

sical music, but especially alternative streams that are well received: jazz, cabaret, outdoor events, revues, and children's theatre. The opera festival in neighbouring Bregenz is unique. During the Festival, a ship sails there daily and docks right at the lakeside stage.

When one considers all the activities and events this city has to offer, plus its unique location and Mediterranean flair, the natural hospitality of the local residents and the cosy pubs and restaurants, it is easy to understand why the Romantic Hölderlin raved about "blissful Lindau".

Through the Reutin and Zech sections of the city, Bregrenzer Straße follows the railway line for the most part, reaching the Austrian frontier at the Leiblach.

A view of Lindau with the towers of St. Stephen's Church and the Collegiate Church.

▲ The Pfänder (1064) affords a magnificent view of the lake.
▼ Good food and drink are available at "Berghaus Pfänder".

The Birds of Prey Flight Demonstration takes place at the Eagle Observation Point just below the mountain station of the Pfänder Railway. This approx. 40 minute demonstration lets you experience birds of prey in free flight in the upwind of the Pfänder Slope. During the summer season, demonstrations are held daily at 11:00 AM and 2.30 PM.

▲ *Mountain railway arrival.*

◀ *Steinbock.   White-headed sea eagle.* ▼

9

Bregenz

Just on the other side of the border and a little before Bregenz is Lochau (population 5800) on Bregenz Bay. All that remains of the one-time rulers of Lochau, the von Raitenau family, are the Alt-Hofen ruins (13. cen.) and the Renaissance-era

Hofen Castle (1585/1616), which today is a centre for science and continuing education and is also used for spa events. In addition to the lakeside swimming centre, Lochau also has kilometres of bathing beaches in both directions. A narrow,

Bregenz on Lake Constance, above it the wide Rhine Valley and mountains of Switzerland with the mighty massif of the Säntis Mountain Chain.

Information

Bregenz Tourist Office, Bahnhofstraße 14, A-6900 Bregenz, phone 05574/49590, fax 495969, international dialling code from Germany (0043).
Vorarlberg State Museum: daily 9:00 - 12:00 AM - noon and 2:00 - 5:00 PM, (closed Monday not during festival season). Vorarlberg Military Museum in the Martinsturm: Good Friday - first Monday after Easter and May - September, 9:00 AM - 6:00 PM; (closed Mondays not during festival season).
Bregenz Art Museum: daily 10:00 AM - 6:00 PM, Thursday until 9:00 PM (closed Monday, not during festival season)

twisting road (7 km) leads by way of Buchenberg to the Pfänder (1064 m), the most famous mountain vantage point over Lake Constance. Of course, one can also hike to the top (1 1/2 - 2 hours from either Lochau or Bregenz) or reach the top within 6 minutes by cable car from Bregenz. The spectacular view over Bregenz and Lake Constance attracts many visitors, especially in summer, so the first cable car line was built in 1927. Today, its modern successor can transport 800 persons per hour in each direction. It is then only a 5-minute walk from the mountain station to the summit. For avid hikers, this is the ideal starting point for a tour of the Bregenzer Wald ("Bregenz Forest"), which is crisscrossed by many marked trails. One especially attractive route is the Käse-Wan-derweg ("Cheese Hiking Path") with a route devoted to learning about cheese and many opportunities to taste the goods at farms, dairies, and inns along the way. It starts here on the Pfänder and leads along the Pfänder ridge all the way to Eichenberg and Möggers. Less athletic persons are especially attracted to the Alpine Wildlife Park with a forest education path and the Adlerwarte ("Eagle's Aerie", flight displays), even if the majority of the guests come because of the magnificent view of the lake. The view is also especially enjoyable from "Berghaus Pfänder" next to the mountain cable car station. The inns "Pfänderdohle", "Pfän-derspitze" or "Schweden-schanze" also ensure that no one goes hungry or thirsty. In the winter, provided there is enough snow, the area is very

❶ *Statehouse;* ❷ *Town Hall;* ❸ *Post Office;* ❹ *Festival and Convention Hall;* ❺ *Theater am Kornmarkt;* ❻ *Vorarlberg State Museum;* ❼ *Thurn and Taxis Arts Centre;* ❽ *Old Town Hall;* ❾ *Federal Office of Monuments;* ❿ *Deuringschlössle;* ⓫ *Martinsturm;* ⓬ *St. Martin's Church;* ⓭ *St. Gallus Parish Church;* ⓮ *Lake Chapel;* ⓳ *Sacred Heart Church;* ⓴ *Nepomuk Chapel;* ㉑ *Mehrerau Abbey;* ㉒ *Capuchin Monastery;* ㉔ *Roman excavations (Brigantium).*

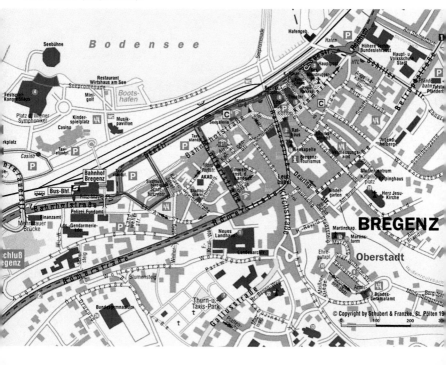

The Bregenz Festival: The set of Beethoven's opera "Fidelio" (1995) on the famous lakeside stage.

popular with skiers, since it has two lifts and permits downhill runs as far as Lochau or Bregenz.

At the foot of the Pfändermassiv, Bregenz is nestled in a semi-circular slope at the Eastern end of Lake Constance. It is because of this much-vaunted location that the town was settled so early; evidence of human habitation has been found from as early as the Bronze Age (3000 years ago). Around 15 BC, the Alpine Rhine Valley and its Celtic population were subjugated by the Roman legions. Under the name of Brigantium, the booming village gained greater importance as a centre of commerce and transportation. After the fall of the frontier fort (3rd cen.), the upper part of the city was fortified. The Alemanians settled here 200 years later. In the 10th cen., the Counts of Bregenz erected their ancestral castle here. Around 1160, both the castle and control over the city went to the Counts of Montfort. Under the Hapsburgs (from 1523), Bregenz experienced a period of revitalisation; it has belonged to Austria ever since. Having first been selected as the centre of the nation's defences due to its favourable location in the tri-national area, the city became the seat of the provincial legislature in 1861 and the provincial capital of Vorarlberg in 1919.

In Bregenz too, our tour of the remarkable city starts at the lakeside in the harbour. The Hafengebäude (harbour building), which has a canopy that runs all the way around the building and once permitted direct transfers from ship to train and vice versa, is already more than 100 years old. The western breakwater has been expanded into a lakeside promenade. Passing the boat harbour (gondola harbour) and the music pavilion as well as the casino and an attached hotel, we come to the festival and convention hall (1980). Its extended "lakeside stage" becomes the focal point of the theatrical world for four weeks every year in July and August. There is room in the stands for 5600 spectators; the "floating stage" is the largest in the world. In the lakeshore area, the Lakeside Swimming Centre adjoins to the west; further inland, an indoor pool and Lake Constance Stadium adjoin. If we continue to follow the beach path, after passing the sporting harbour we ultimately reach the yacht harbour. Between these two harbour basins, a path leads inland to the Cistercian Abbey of Mehrerau. Regrettably, little is left of buildings erected by the founders of the abbey, a group of Benedictine monks (11th cen.). The Romanesque church and the Baroque reconstruction of 1743 were followed by a neo-Romanesque sanctuary, which was forced in turn to make way for a concrete structure in 1960. The foundations of the original abbey church can still be seen in the crypt.

Our tour of the Unterstadt or "Lower City" starts at the lakeside promenade again, first leading us along the Seestraße to the Kunsthaus (Art Museum) opened in 1997. This building, the largest museum built in Austria since World War II, holds contemporary art, architecture, and design. It is adjoined by the neo-classical Post Office Building, which was built in 1900 as a sign of the importance of the city (which had 6000 inhabitants at the time) as the western outpost of the Danube monarchy of the time. Behind it is the Nepomuk Chapel (Nepomukkapelle, 1757), a sanctuary used by the Hungarian congregation. The Rococo-style ro-

tunda is adorned by a harmoniously sweeping cupola topped with a skylight turret, a depiction of the patron saint of the church over the portal, and inside, scenes from the saint's life. The Baroque inn "Gasthaus zum Kornmesser" is somewhat older (1720). It is the work and one-time residence of Master Builder Franz Anton Beer von Bleichten, who also created the basilica in Weingarten and the Abbey Church in Weissenau.

Via Kornmarktstraße, we pass the "Theatre am Kornmarkt", which was once a grain silo, to come to the Vorarlberger Landesmuseum (Vorarlberg State Museum, 1903, expanded 1956-59). It houses an important collection of artefacts of the earliest historical and prehistoric times, Roman objects from Brigantium, and valuable works from the Gothic, Renaissance, and Baroque periods. Worthy of particular mention are the Roman relief of Epona, the altar pictures by Wolf

Bregenz: Parish Church of St. Gallus (1737/38) with late Gothic tower and Baroque cap.

Bregenz: The massive Martinsturm (1599-1602) and its gigantic, onion-shaped cupola are considered a hallmark of the state capital of Vorarlberg (Austria).

Huber (1521), the Crucifixion group done by Michael Erhart or one of his associates (ca. 1510), and the extensive painting collection of Angelika Kauffmann, the most famous female painter of Vorarlberg at the end of the 18th century.

The nearby Town Hall (Rathaus, 1686) was built at the end of the 19th century in the style of the late Renaissance. It is adjoined by the Lake Chapel of St. George (Seekapelle St. Georg), which was built right after the Town Hall. It stands on the site of an older chapel that was founded to commemorate the Appenzell War (1403-1408).

Following Rathausstraße and Maurachgasse, we reach the once-fortified "upper City" or Oberstadt. Here stands the imposing Martinsturm, a hallmark of the city. It was erected 1599-1602 on the foundations of a grain silo in the medieval castle. The arcades in the upper floor and the gigantic, onion-shaped roof construction are remarkable. In the lower floor is the Martinskapelle, in which a valuable cycle of frescoes (painted starting in 1363) is preserved. A small museum has been set up above this. The Old Town Hall (Alte Rathaus, 1622), a historic half-timbered building, is not far away. The Deuringschlösschen (ca. 1670) on the west corner of the relatively narrow Oberstadt square is a hotel and restaurant today. Outside the Oberstadt are the Cappucine Monastery and St. Gallus' Parish Church. The church's late Gothic tower has a Baroque ridge capping (1672). The nave was not created until 1737/38 (Franz Anton Beer). Immediately thereafter, the high altar, the Rococo stucco and the choir stalls, which evidence remarkable workmanship, were created immediately thereafter.

To the Southeast, the mountain known as Gebhardsberg rises to an altitude of nearly 600 m.

On its summit are the impressive ruins of Hohenbregenz Castle, which was blown up by the Swedes in 1647. The terrace of the castle restaurant affords a magnificent view of Bregenz, Lake Constance, the Rhine Valley and the Alps. In the Wallfahrtskirche ("Pilgrimage Church", 18th cen.) the wall paintings (ca. 1900)

that portray the life of St. Gebhard are especially attractive.

From Bregenz, it is possible to make an outing up into the Rhine Valley, which

Bregenz: Castle ruins and Castle Restaurant atop the scenic outlook Gebhardsberg.

goes by way of Dornbirn (Classical Parish Church of St. Martin, hiking trails through the famous Rappenlochschlucht and the Alploch, Vorarlberg Nature Show), Hohenems (Alt-Ems ruins, Glopper Castle or Neu-Ems, Jewish Museum), and Feldkirch (Gothic Cathedral of St. Nicholas, Schattenburg Castle, historic city centre) to Liechtenstein, the miniature country (population 30,000, ca. 50 km, State Art Collection of the Royal Family, Postal Museum, Walser Museum of Local History) between Austria and Switzerland. Starting at Feldkirch, it is also possible to make a side trip via Bludenz to the Silvretta Reservoir (approx. 100 km from Bregenz).

The Rhine Valley

10

On the other side of the Ache River in Bregenz is the Rhine Valley (Rheintal), which we now cross. Our first stop is **Hard** (pop. 11,800), a one-time fishermen's and farming village between the mouths of the Bregenzer Ache and the new Rhine, which was diverted from its natural course to here (see Old Rhine) in 1900. Hard boasts one of the biggest beach bathing facilities in the Lake Constance region and a beach for nudists. At the lake, it is also possible to go wind surfing (2 schools), sailing, boating (rentals), and fishing. By the way - and perhaps neighbouring countries will follow suit - the entire Austrian lakeshore is open to the public without restriction! The boats of the Austrian Lake Constance Line also anchor in the big harbour. It is

The New Rhine flowing into Lake Constance between Hard and Fußach. At left: the Bregenzer Ache estuary. Above the broad Rhine Valley are the majestic mountains of Vorarlberg.

Bregenz Tourist Office, Bahnhofstraße 14, A-6900 Bregenz, phone 05574/49590, fax 495969, international dialling code from Germany (0043).

Late fall at the Rohrspitze near Höchst.

the home port for the "Hohentwiel", which was built in 1913 and is the last paddle-wheel steamer on the "Swabian Sea".

Across from **Hard,** on the left bank of the Rhine, is the little town of **Fußach** (pop. 3,300), which is more of a residential community than a tourist spot. Nonetheless, with the large nature preserve around Rohrspitz (New Rhine) and Rheinspitz (Old Rhine), it has a unique attraction that draws numerous nature lovers from Austria, Germany, and Switzerland, especially on the weekends. This sedimentation zone of the Rhine Delta measures 2000 ha, making it the largest freshwater delta in Europe. It is home to around 300 species and valuable biosphere for rare plants and native birds, as well as being an important spring and fall resting place for many migratory birds.

Around two miles south of Fußach is **Höchst** (pop.7,000), just a little below the spot were the manmade bed of the New Rhine branches off from the old riverbed. Water still flows in the Old Rhine, even if it is only a fraction of the original volume. That is advantageous for the settlements in the delta, which used to be plagued by destructive floods at regular intervals. The Old Rhine flows in winding curves past Höchst and later Gaißau, before it flows into Lake Constance at the Rheinspitz.

The border town of **St. Margrethen** is a railway centre and customs transshipment centre. This popular spa and shopping town in Eastern Switzerland is not only the home of the famous mineral spring, but also has valuable historical buildings that are relics of its heyday in the Middle Ages. In particular, sights worth seeing include the Cemetery Chapel of St. Margaretha (mentioned 1090, present-day structure dates mostly from around 1300) with its frescoes and late Gothic altars, the ruins of Grimmenstein Castle, and Heldsberg Castle (castle museum).

From St. Margrethen it is approx. 12 km to Rorschach, the next stop on our tour of Lake Constance.

Idyll in the Rhine delta.

Rorschach

11

Passing the fishing village Altenrhein via the Staad area of the town, we reach the main town of Rorschach (pop. 10,000). It was founded by the Alemannians way back in the 7th century as a Lake Constance harbour serving, in particular, the important Abbey of St. Gall. Under the influence of the Abbey, the settlement was granted market, mint, and customs rights by King Otto I. In the 15th century, trading in grain was especially important, later also trading with canvases from Upper Swabia. Upon dissolution of the Abbey, Rorschach was assigned to the Canton of St. Gallen in 1803.

The centre of economic life is the expansive federal railway harbour, over which towers the mighty granary (1746/49), probably one of the loveliest and most impressive of its kind in Switzerland. Today, some of the rooms house a museum of local history and an art collection. The harbour premises also include the customs office and - on the other side of the railway line - the harbour railway station. To the east it is adjoined by the well-groomed lakeside park, through which the lakeside promenade leads down to the yacht harbour. A little farther inland, Churer Straße leads us back in the direction of the city centre again. Stately patrician houses from the 18th century, adorned with decorative bays, bear eloquent witness to the period of economic prosperity. The Baroque Catholic parish Church of St. Columbian (1645-1667, south of Town

Museum "Alte Garage": a Packard 901 (1932) and a Bentley 4¼ litre (1936) (from right).

Tourist office, CH-9400 Rorschach, Switzerland, phone: 071/18417034, fax 8417036, international calling code from Germany (0041).
Museum in Kornhaus: *for groups only, by appointment, phone: 071/8417034.*
Automobile, Motorcycle, and Automatic Machine Museum "Alte Garage": *March - June and September - November, Monday - Friday 1:30 - 5:30 PM, Saturday 1:30 - 5:30 PM, Sunday 10:00 AM - 5:30 PM; July + August, Monday - Sunday 10:00 AM - 6:00 PM.*

Rorschach: A magnificent Renaissance double bay window (1650) on one of the stately patrician houses, the Weber House.

Hall) and especially the one-time Benedictine Mariaberg Abbey south of the city are both worth seeing. The Abbey has lovely cloisters. The refectory (dining room) and the chapter halls (meeting place) with important frescoes have been preserved from the time when the abbey was founded (ca. 1500). Since secularisation nearly 200 years ago, the building has been used as a teacher's college. Thus the highly traditional port became a community uniting the elements of an industrial and shopping town as well as a centre of tourism and education.

Rorschach is also a good starting point for day trips. From the St.-Anna-Schloß ("St. Anne's Palace"), above Mariaberg, a hiking path leads in an hour to the mountain outlook Rossbüchel (964 m) with the nearby "Fünfländerblick" ("View of the Five Countries"). Sulzberg Palace (tower, 13th cen.) and Wartegg Palace (1557, lovely park, refuge of the Austrian Imperial family following the dissolution of the monarchy in 1919 and prior to their banishment to the Island of Madeira) are in the immediate vicinity of Rorschach.

St. Gallen

The capital of the Canton of St. Gallen is 10 km away from Lake Constance, but it is an absolute must-see attraction for culturally aware vacationers here, if only for its historical sights. St. Gallen, the population of which has grown to 71,000, is an administrative and industrial centre (textiles and metal-working), a cultural stronghold, and the most important shopping and trade-fair city in Eastern Switzerland. It owes its origin to the hermitage of the itinerant Irish monk Gall, which he founded here in 612 and which evolved into an abbey (ca. 720) with a village of craftsmen. In the 9th - 11th cen., the Benedictine Abbey was at the zenith of its importance due to its school and, above all, its library. The Abbots were made princes of the realm in 1207. They kept this title until secularisation in 1805. The one-time craftsmen's village was chartered as a city in the 10th cen. and was accorded the status of a free imperial city in 1212. The city allied itself with the Swiss confederation in 1454 and permanently renounced its allegiance to the prince-bishops three years later. In the 13th - 20th centuries, textile processing (linen and cotton weaving, embroidery) made the city one of the most affluent ones for miles around.

The library of the former Benedictine Abbey is world famous. The Rococo hall with its elaborate inlaid floor, the fine stucco work (by the Gigl brothers) and the splendid frescoes (Joseph Wannenmacher, subjects include the ecumenical church councils of the 4th and 5th centuries, four Eastern Fathers of the Church, and four Western Fathers of the Church) provide a setting worthy of this important collection. The library owns many 9th - 11th century works that belonged to the former abbey school, where special attention was paid to translation from Latin into Alemannian as well as literary arts and book illumination. One-of-a-kind holdings include, for example, the "Psalterium Aureum" (9th. cen.), the "Casus Sancti Galli" (11th cen.), a manuscript of the Nibelungenlied (13th cen.), and an abbey plan drawn up on parchment (9th cen.) according to the Rules of St. Benedict.

Other attractions on display include a mummy from Northern Egypt that lies in a double sarcophagus made of fig-tree wood. Today the library holds a total of approximately 150,000 volumes, over 2000 mostly rare manuscripts, and more than 1600 incunabula (books printed in the early days of printing before 1520).

The impressive abbey buildings (17th/18th cen.) are grouped around a wide abbey courtyard and today are used as work-

St. Gallen Tourist Information, Bahnhofplatz 1 a, CH-9001 St. Gallen, Switzerland. Phone: 071/2273737, fax: 2273767, international dialling code from Germany (0041). Abbey Library: April - beginning of November, Monday - Saturday 9:00 - 12:00 AM - noon and 1:30 - 5:00 PM. Sunday 10:00 - 12:00 AM - noon and 1:30 - 4:00 PM. Beginning of December - March, Monday - Saturday 9:00 - 12:00 AM - noon and 1:30 - 4:00 PM.
Historical Museum, Museum of Nature, Art Museum, Museum in Kirchhofer Haus: Tuesday - Saturday, 10:00 - 12:00 AM - noon, 2:00 - 5:00 PM; Sunday 10:00 AM - 5:00 PM, closed Mondays. **Textile Museum:** Monday - Friday 10:00 - 12:00 AM - noon, 2:00 - 5:00 PM; Saturday (April - Oct.) 10:00 - 12:00 AM - noon, 2:00 - 5:00 PM, closed Sundays and holidays.

St. Gallen: The late Baroque Abbey Church of Sts. Gall and Otmar, built 1755-1766 under the famous master builder Peter Thumb.

space by the bishops, the clergy attached to the cathedral, and the government of the Canton. The present-day meeting room for the Grand Council was once the throne room of the prince-bishops. In addition to the aforementioned library, this building also houses the Abbey Archives with more than 20,000 documents. The inside of the late Baroque cathedral, one of the last monumental late Baroque buildings, is especially ornate. It was designed 1755-1766 as a collegiate church by Peter Thumb, who was also responsible for designing the Library Hall. The stucco work in the choir and the ceiling paintings were also done by the same artists who were responsible for the gold choir grating and the ornately carved cheeks of the choir stalls (scenes from the life of St. Benedict): artist Joseph Anton Feuchtmayer of Wessobrunn, reliefs by the Freiburg sculptor Christian Wenzinger. The crypt of the former collegiate church, in which the bishops of St. Gallen are buried, is considerably older (10th cen.). South of the abbey, the city's defences ran the course of the former city wall, is west of the abbey. The Textile Museum is in Vadianstraße, which branches off of Obere Graben. This museum exhibits especially exquisite embroidery and lace dating from the 15th century on, as well as old pattern books from local shops and Egyptian burial artefacts. The Broderbrunnen, a symbol of the Lake Constance water supply, which was already operational in 1894 in St.. Gallen, also stands in the street Obere Graben. At Schibener Tor, we turn right and

St. Gallen: The world-famous library of the former Benedictine abbey, with magnificent stucco work and frescoes, as well as an intricate inlaid floor.

very close to the abbey walls. Here the Karlstor (ca. 1570) and a round tower have been preserved; a little further out is the Müllertor. Further westward, a square, a memorial, and a street commemorate the city's namesake patron, St. Gall. There are still many historic patrician houses, with typical, richly decorated bay windows, here and there along the adjoining alleys. Obere Graben, a gently arching street that marks come to the Marktplatz ("Marketplace") with a monument to "Vadian". "Vadian", whose real name was Joachim von Watt, was born in St. Gallen and made a name for himself as a Humanist and Reformer. He was friends with Zwingli and corresponded with Luther. For many years, starting in 1526, he was mayor of his hometown and introduced the Reformation here. The city library, which is known as the "Vadiana", is also named after him. Although clearly dwarfed by its famous sister library at the abbey, this collection of 660,000 books and 2,400 manuscripts is the perfect complement to its sister library, especially since the Vadiana contains many materials relating to the Reformation.

Another square, called the "Bohl", begins at the market place just on the other side of Marktgasse. The Waaghaus, which marks the beginning of the Museumsstraße (literally "the street of museums"), is located in the extension of this square. St. Gallen's temples of culture are scattered throughout the city park to right and left of the street. On the right are the City Theatre, the Museum of Natural History and Art (1877; minerals, evolution of life; artworks from the 19th/20th cen.) and the Museum of History (pre-history, history and ethnology, collections primarily from Canton St. Gallen). On the left are the concert house or "Tonhalle", the Museum at Kirchhoferhaus (artefacts recovered from caves, objets d'art, collections of coins and silver) and, set back against Notkerstraße, the aforementioned library. Numerous other works of art are in the possession of the University for Economics and Social Sciences, where they can be admired inside and in front of the university buildings.

Worthwhile destinations for daytrips outside the city include the Freudenberg (3 km south, majestic view of the city, Lake Constance, and the Säntis mountain chain), the "Peter and Paul" Wildlife Preservation Area (3.5 km north) or the Säntispark Shopping and Recreation Centre (indoor and outdoor sports and bathing facilities). Trips to Teufen (7 km southeast, charming village square with a church and a museum) and Bühler (2 km farther, pretty Appenzell houses) are also attractive.

An aerial view of downtown St. Gallen, dominated by the enormous buildings of the famous abbey.

Arbon

13

On the way from Rorschach to Arbon (6.5 km), we pass the two scenicly situated little towns of Horn and Steinach. In the old fishing village of Steinach, which is situated on the stream of the same name, there are two historic buildings: the Baroque Pfarrkirche St. Jakobus ("Parish Church of St. Jacob", 18th cen.) and the enormous Kornhaus (1473).

Steinach is situated on a small peninsula, while neighbouring Arbon is situated on a larger one. The city received its name from the Celts (Arbona); the name was later adopted by the Romans (Arbor Felix). The Romans built a fort here in the 3rd cen. AD, on the foundations of which a castle already stood in the Romanesque period. The palace of the bishops of Constance has stood in its place since 1515; it was occupied by the bishops and their officials until around 1800. Today, Arbon (pop. approx. 13,000) is the third largest city in canton Thurgau.

A manmade dike with numerous parking spaces and a landing pier divides the harbour basin into the Old Harbour and the

Arbon: The Römerhof (ca. 1500) stands at the west end of the Hauptstraße.

Information

Tourist office, Bahnhofstraße 40, CH-9320 Arbon, Switzerland, phone: 071/ 4478515, fax: 4478510, international calling code from Germany (0041).
Palace Historical Museum: May - September, daily 2:00 - 5:00 PM; October, November, March, and April, Sundays only, 2:00 - 5:00 PM.

Palace Harbour. A street leads past the Customs Office to the Church of St. Martin. In the shadow of this church stands the much older Chapel of St. Gall (ca. 1000) with frescoes from the early 14th century. At the entrance to the chapel is a stone with footprints. According to legend, these are the footprints of St. Gall, who, while preaching in Arbon, wrestled with the devil incarnate in the form of a bear.

One of the city's proudest historic patrician houses, the Rote Haus ("Red House", 18th cen.), stands across from the church. Together with the two aforementioned houses of worship, the Palace of the prince-bishops of Constance forms the basis of the historic city centre, which fans out from here into the hinterland. Today, the palace houses a museum of local history and an adult education centre. The Landenbergsaal, a hall dating from the time when the palace was built (1515) under Bishop Hugo von Hohenlandenberg, is especially worth seeing.

There are other interesting buildings, particularly in the Hauptstraße: the house "Zur Straußenfeder" and the "Stadthaus" are two magnificent examples that served as stores during the golden age of the linen business (17th / 18th cen.). The "Römerhof" on the other hand, which is farther down the Hauptstraße evolved from a former defensive tower, as did the Rathaus (Town Hall, 1791) at the end of Rathausgasse. There are many other remarkable buildings besides these, for example: the house "Zur Torwache", the "Kappeli", the Turmhaus or "Tower House" (all 14th / 15th cen.) and the house "Zum Storchen".

The city is especially proud of its extensive lakeshore promenade. Here there is room for a large, heated pool, a bathing beach and a nature beach, sailing, surfing, and water-skiing, atmospheric strolling, tennis, camping, a fitness course, and a BMX track on which the annual Swiss National Championships are held. Galleries, a mineralogical collection, and three museums (Museum of History, Classic Cars Museum, Juice and Distillery Museum) round out the palette of available pastimes in this active Lake Constance community.

Arbon: A view of the Old Harbour and the Church of St. Martin. In front of its choir (1490) is the Chapel of St. Gall.

Romanshorn

14

Romanshorn is just 9 km north-west of Arbon at the place where the Aach flows into Lake Constance. Mentioned in official documents as early as 779, the town owes its importance mainly to its easily accessible location on the shore of Lake Constance and at the end of a long valley that permits good connections to Winterthur and Zurich. The harbour from 1841 was already expanded into a ferry harbour upon completion of the railway line (1855). In 1911, this harbour handled more than 80,000 freight cars on their way to and from Friedrichshafen. Especially after World War II, however, transshipment declined steadily until it was discontinued, for lack of profit-ability, in 1976. Today the ferries only carry passengers and their cars on the 16 km route at the widest point on the Upper Lake, taking some 40 minutes to do so.

Romanshorn is the most important transportation hub on the Swiss shore and has the largest harbour on Lake Constance, the home port and shipyard for the ships of the Swiss Lake Constance Line. Nonetheless, the town has also evolved into a holiday paradise in the past few decades. Generously dimensioned quays north and south of the harbour allow plenty of room for visitors' boats. The adjacent, well-groomed parks permit an enjoyable stroll.

The only historical buildings in the locali-

Romanshorn: A historic half-timbered house.

Information

Tourist Office, Bahnhof, CH- 8590 Romanshorn, Switzerland, phone: 071/4633232, fax: 4612330, international calling code from Germany (0041).
"The Little Museum at the Harbour": *May - October, Sunday 2:00 - 5:00 PM. July/August also Saturdays 2:00 - 5:00 PM.*

ty to survive several devastating 18th century blazes are located next to the northern lake park. The Palace was built in 1829; today it is a hotel. The nearby "Old Church", which is dedicated to Saints Mary, Peter, and Gall, is largely representative of the Gothic style, but also has Romanesque elements dating from the time of original construction.

The shore-promenade takes us past the northern boat-harbour to a vantage point giving us a good view of the "Inseli," a by the varied playground equipment. Fine food and drink and a broad palette of possible day trips by rail, bus, car or ship further increase the recreational value of this friendly holiday spot.

A side trip to Amriswil, 7 km from Lake Constance, takes us to the stately half-timbered house "Zum Bären" and the (likewise half-timbered) "Altes Pfarrhaus" ("Old Parsonage", 1672, now a museum of local history). Just 3 km away from here is Hagenwil, where visitors can see a mag-

Romanshorn: A view over the Swiss Rail Harbour to the Catholic church.

boulder in the sea, to the mini-golf course, and to the attractive swimming pool. Besides many other opportunities to use one's leisure time in an active way, there are numerous bicycling routes and hiking paths along the lake or, for example, to heavily frequented forest taverns, where adults fortify themselves with food and drink, while children are entertained mainly nificently renovated former moated castle (13th cen., castle chapel, Gothic knights' hall). On the way to Münsterlingen (14 km), we pass through the small vacation spot known as Uttwil, the tranquillity and seclusion of which have already attracted many artists, and Kesswil, where visitors can look forward to seeing numerous ornate half-timbered houses.

Münsterlingen

Before we reach the little town of Münsterlingen, let us stop briefly in **Landschlacht** (pop. 850). The attractions in this peaceful holiday spot include the pretty half-timbered inn "Rotes Haus" and the house "Zur Sonne". An absolute "must" for visitors, however, is the Leonhardskapelle ("St. Leonhard's Chapel", 10th cen.), which is decorated with interesting frescoes. The sequence of pictures in the choir (15th cen.) portrays the life of the patron saint of the church, while those on the south wall (14th cen.) of the nave depict scenes from the passion of Christ. This vacation town has a bathing beach, a campground, a sailing and yacht school, and tennis courts.

The next bathing beach is in Münsterlingen, a part of Scherzingen at the entrance to the "Constance Funnel". From here on, the Upper Lake narrows in the form of a bay between the Swiss shore and the "Bodanrücken" until reaching the "Seerhein", which widens again below Constance into the Lower Lake. One sight that is definitely worth seeing is

Münsterlingen Abbey Church: The bust of St. John is the focal point of a rare procession.

For information on Münsterlingen, contact: Tourist Office, CH-8280 Kreuzlingen, phone 071/6723840, fax 6723840, international calling code from Germany (0041). Kornschütte Lake Museum in Kreuzlingen: April - October, Wednesday, Saturday, Sunday 2:00 - 5:00 PM; November - March, each Sunday of every month, 2:00 - 5:00 PM.

the abbey complex of the former Benedictine convent, which sits on a hill above the town and the lake. The rewards of a visit are not only the view, but also a tour of the church interior. It is the work of the famous master builder Franz Beer von Bleichten, who fit it into the North Wing of the complex in 1709. Over the main portal is the great nuns' gallery. The rather reserved, pure white stucco emphasises the colourful frescoes as well as the altars and the choir grating, which emerge in an especially plastic manner. The bust of St. John the Evangelist (16. cen.) is currently kept in the Abbey Church. In keeping with an old custom, the likeness switches locations between the Parish Church in Hagnau and the local Abbey Church with every "Seegfrörne": i.e., whenever Lake Constance is completely frozen over. It has stood here since 9 February 1963, after being carried in a solemn procession from the German shore over the ice. Today the abbey buildings house a psychiatric clinic.

Continuing our journey to Constance, we pass the little town of Bottighofen (pop. 900), which is home to a great mill, a modern boat harbour, and a romantic palace hotel. A charming lakeshore path leads from here to the sister cities of Kreuzlingen (Switzerland) and Constance (Germany).

Procession from Hagnau to Münsterlingen across the ice of the Upper Lake. Historic photograph taken on 9 February 1963, the date of the heretofore last "Seegfrörne".

69

Constance

Kreuzlingen, the last Swiss town on the Upper Lake, was once a district of Constance. The extensive lakeside grounds and the majestic old trees are certainly worth a look. Right between them stands, like a fairytale castle, the Seeburg, the

former summer residence of the bishops of Constance. Built in 1598 and destroyed in the century thereafter, the complex was rebuilt in idealised romantic form in the 19th century. Nearby stands the former granary of the monastery, which is now a

Constance on Lake Constance: Here the "Seerhein" leaves Upper Lake Constance to re-enter a few kilometres to the west in Lower Lake Constance. The part of the city known as Petershausen is to the right.

Information

Tourist-Information Constance GmbH, Fischmarkt 2, D-78462 Constance, phone: 07531/1330-30, fax 1330-60.
Rosgarten Museum: *Tuesday - Thursday 10:00 AM - 5:00 PM, Friday - Sunday 10:00 AM - 4:00 PM.* **Hus Museum:** *Tuesday - Sunday 10:00 AM - 12:00 noon, 2:00 PM - 4:00 PM. May - Sept. Tuesday - Sunday 10:00 AM - 12.30 noon, 1:30 PM - 5:00 PM.* **Lake Constance Museum of Natural History:** *Tuesday - Thursday 10:00 AM - 5:00 PM, Friday - Sunday 10:00 AM - 4:00 PM.* **State Museum of Archaeology:** *Tuesday - Sunday 10:00 AM - 6:00 PM.* **Sea Life Centre:** *Off season 10:00 AM - 6:00 PM, High season 10:00 AM - 9:00 PM, open every day except on 24th Dec.*

lake museum. It provides information about shipping, tourism, trade, fishing, and the study of rivers and lakes in a vivid manner.

The German border runs, seemingly at random, through the middle of the neighbourhoods.

There were already pile buildings in Con-stance Bay way back in 2000 BC. In the 2nd cen. AD, the Celts settled on the highest point within the modern city, the present Münsterhügel ("Cathedral Hill"). The Romans erected a fortified village at this strategically favourable location in the 3rd cen. AD; in the 4th cen. they named it "Constantia" in honour of their Emperor (Con-

❶ *Council Building;* ❷ *Market;* ❸ *Rosgartenmuseum;* ❹ *Church of the Holy Trinity;* ❺ *Schnetztor;* ❻ *Town Hall;* ❼ *Haus zum Hohen Hafen;* ❽ *Hohes Haus;* ❾ *Church of St. Stephen;* ❿ *Cathedral;* ⓫ *Jesuit Church;* ⓬ *Rheintorturm;* ⓭ *Powder Tower;* ⓮ *Island Hotel*

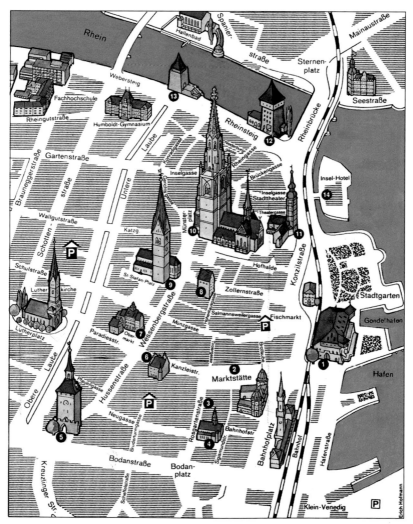

Constance:
The Medieval Schnetz-
tor (at left) and the
Gothic bay windows
of the house
"Zum Elefanten".

stantius Chlorus). As "Constenz", the village became a bishopric (6th cen.) and soon evolved into an important centre for the production and trading of linen. Because it was located at the intersection of several important trade routes, the city became the scene of one the largest and most important gatherings of the Middle Ages, the "Council of Constance" (1414-18). During this council, the only one ever held on German soil, the city of then approx. 7000 inhabitants hosted more than 70,000 visitors from countries all over Europe. The council, which met in the cathedral, had set out to reform and unite the then divided church. Among the invited guests was the Reformer and Rector of the University of Prague, Jan Hus. Despite assurances of free passage given by King Sigismund,

who was also present, Hus was arrested, sentenced for heresy, and burned alive outside the city (in the modern district of the city known as Paradies). His follower Jerome of Prague, who had come after Hus to support him, fared no better the following year. The three popes and antipopes of that time, ensconced in Rome, Pisa, and Avignon respectively, were removed from power, one after other. In November 1417, a new pope was elected in the store at the harbour, which is called the "Council Building" today. Martin V remains the only pope ever elected on German soil.

At the waning of the Middle Ages, Constance's fortunes also declined. In the wake of a bitter defeat in the "Swabian War" (1499), the city lost control of the Kreuzlingen district, which allied itself with

Switzerland. In 1526, the bishopric was moved to Meersburg, and the city was stripped of its sovereignty in the Schmalkaldic War (1548). The city belonged to Austria for the next 250 years. The economic decline was even more severe, because trade routes shifted to the harbours in Northern Germany after the discovery of the New World. Constance was annexed to Baden in 1805. With the start of tourism (steamship 1824, railway 1863, airport 1918, car-ferry 1928) the regained some of its earlier importance, especially as it was spared from bombing attacks in World War II because of its proximity to neutral Switzerland. In this way, all of the city's historical buildings were preserved. The University of Constance was founded in 1966. Today the university, which has a student body numbering over 10,000, is one of the most important employers in the city.

Our tour through this highly historical city starts at the harbour, where travellers arrive by ferry, excursion boat, or ship as well as by rail or car (there are parking spaces at the harbour and on Bodanstraße). Along the harbour basin (19th cen.), the home port of the German Rail Fleet, we pass the Harbour Customs Office and Tourist Information Office and come to the landing that marks the northern end of the harbour. At its tip are the Constance water gauge and a gigantic female figure, the "Imperia". This work by artist Peter Lenk from Bodman - which is 9 m tall and weighs 18 tonnes - symbolises the power of the courtesans who followed the male participants to Constance by the hundreds at the time of the Council of Constance. In her hands, Imperia holds the naked, dwarf-like figures of King Sigismund and Pope Martin V. The provocatively clad woman on the base of the former light tower turns continually about her own axis, so that every visitor gets a view of her well-proportioned front sooner or later. While it is understandable that this work of art unleashed heated

Constance: Harbour entrance with the gigantic statue "Imperia": In the background is the city's most famous building, the historic "Council Building".

debate following its 1993 unveiling, it has since become one of the city's landmarks. North of the landing is the little Gondelhafen ("Gondola Harbour") with an obelisk commemorating the famous Count Ferdinand von Zeppelin, the inventor of the eponymous airship. The stately building on the inland side of the Gondelhafen is really a former store, but it is known as the **"Council Building" ❶**. This is where the 1417 papal election was held during the council. Fifty-three cardinals and del-

house "Zum roten Korb". At the end of the square is the Kaiserbrunnen ("Fountain of the Emperors") which bears not only the busts of three emperors, but also gargoyle "rabbit seals" and an eight-legged horse that has surprised many a visitor.

Just after the fountain we turn left onto Rosgartenstraße. The Medieval guildhouse of the butchers, named **"Zum Rosgarten" ❸**, has been turned into a **museum** of the same name. It contains collections pertaining to the history of the

Constance: The only papal election on German soil was held in the historic Council Building in 1417.

egates were sequestered here for three days until they finally agreed on the Italian Cardinal Oddone Colonna, who took the name of Pope Martin V.

An underground passageway near the historic building brings us to the **market in the heart ❷** of the historic city centre. The pleasant patrician houses include two remarkable specimens: the former inn "Gasthof zum Goldenen Adler" and the

city as well as art and culture in the Lake Constance region. On display are artefacts from the cave known as the "Kesslerloch", artefacts of the pile dwelling culture and art objects from the city's Medieval heyday. After going a little farther, we encounter the Gothic **Church of the Holy Trinity ❹**, built ca. 1300 as a monastery church for the Augustinians. The interior fell prey to the "iconoclasts"

Constance: Peter Lenk's statue "Imperia" turns at the entrance to the harbour.

of the 16th century, so the only remnants of Middle Ages are the frescoes painted around the time of the council. Later, this otherwise all too plain church was decorated with Baroque stucco and handsome altars from Einsiedeln.

One cross street back again, the Obere Augustinergasse leads us to a square known as Blätzeplatz. On the square is a fountain of the same name, dedicated to a figure that is typical of Mardi Gras in Constance, the "Blätzlebuebe." In the extension of the alley we come to Hussenstraße. The **Schnetztor** ❺ (14th cen.) at the end of this street marks the course of the former city wall. Today the nearby Hushaus ("Hus House", ca. 1500) is a memorial to the Bohemian reformer, who was executed here in Constance on 6 July

1415. He is still honoured as a martyr today with flowers that are laid at the Hussenstein ("Huss' Stone", approx. 400 m to the west on Döbelestraße). Going back along Hussenstraße, we come to the Obermarkt ("Upper Market") at the Malhaus (ca. 1400, it has been an apothecary's ever since then), which is also where public executions were held in the early Middle Ages. The Upper Market and the marketplace were connected by a pergola in the 12th century. This is roughly the course followed by the modern-day Kanzleigasse, which we follow on a side trip to the **Town Hall** ❻. Before it was converted into a town hall (in the 16th cen.), the building (14th cen.) served as the guildhouse of the linen weavers and shopkeepers. Today the

*Constance:
A tranquil rest
at the market-
place.*

romantic, Renaissance-style Innenhof ("Inner Court") is a venue for serenade concerts during the summer months.

As we continue along Hussenstraße, we pass the **"Haus zum Hohen Hafen"**  (ca. 1420). Its murals (ca. 1900) relate

Constance: The stately Town Hall was built in the 14th century as the guild-hall of the shopkeepers and linen weavers.

events having to do with the Council of Constance. Back then, it was in front of this house that King Sigismund granted the Burgrave of Nuremberg, Friedrich IV, the Brandenburg March as a fiefdom. Next door is the Hotel "Barbarossa", which has been an inn since at least 1419. Its name is derived from an even earlier historical event, for it was on this square that Emperor Friedrich I "Barbarossa" made peace with the Lombard cities in 1183.

roque organ, a "Moon Crescent Madonna", and three reliefs with motives from the story of the passion. A look diagonally across the Stephansplatz ("St. Stephen's Square") reveals the balcony of the former Franciscan monastery, from which Friedrich Hecker proclaimed (in vain) the first German Republic on 12 April 1848.

Wessenbergstraße takes us past the choir of the Church of St. Stephen and further northward to Wessenberghaus.

Constance: The modern Hotel "Barbarossa" was already an inn in 1419.

Now we turn right onto Münzgasse and left again right away onto Hohenhausgasse. Even before we reach the next street corner, on the left-hand side we find the tower residence "Zum goldenen Löwen" (ca. 1450) in a backyard. The murals are from the 16th century. Up ahead in the alley stands the **Hohe Haus** ❽ (1294), which also has five storeys, but in which the frescoes are from a more recent time. Here we turn left onto Zollerngasse, which takes us to the late Gothic **Church of St. Stephen** ❾ (1424-1486, built on a Romanesque foundation). The sights worth seeing here are, above all, the choir stalls richly adorned with fabulous creatures (ca. 1300 and 1430), the tabernacle (1594), the Ba-

The building was created in its present form in 1617, when several smaller, older buildings were combined under one roof. The most prominent resident of the house was Baron von Wessenberg, who was Vicar General and Diocesan Administrator beginning in 1803. Today this building houses a sales room belonging to the Spital Wine Cellars and the Wessenberg Gallery. The latter hosts rotating exhibitions of masterpieces of the 16th - 20th centuries, by, among others, Rembrandt, Titian, Raffael, Tintoretto and Dürer. The city library is housed in the upper floors of the building, the art association is in the annexe.

Across the street stands the **Münster "Unserer Lieben Frau zu Konstanz"** ❿

("Saint Mary's Cathedral in Constance") with its 76 m high tower, to the south in front of it, the slim Mariensäule (Column of Saint Mary, 1683) stretches skyward. The sanctuary was built starting in 1052 on the site of a collapsed 8th century bishop's church, but was often modified. so that today it contains not only Romanesque, but also Gothic, Baroque, and neo-Gothic elements. Through the tower hall we come to the intriguing main portal. Above its 20 relief representations (1470), one recognises the "Konstanzer Herrgott", a wooden crucifix (1518). The Council met inside the church 1414-1418; this is where Jan Hus was found guilty of heresy. Another reformer, however, cost the church most of its treasures: Ulrich Zwingli, who was ordained to the priesthood here in 1505, permitted his followers to plunder the sanctuary and steal or destroy the valuable furnishings. Nonetheless, there is still plenty to admire: the organ loft just behind the portal, the pulpit (1680), the monolithic Romanesque columns in the nave, the high altar in the choir, and, underneath it, the early Romanesque crypt (10th cen.) with four gold-plated panels (11th-13th cen.), the Golden Panels of Constance. From the high choir we come to the upper vestry, in which a crucifixion scene from 1348 hangs, and the large Chapter Hall (15th cen.). The two rooms mentioned each form the upper storey of the two remaining wings of the former cloisters. At their shared corner is the Mauritius Rotunda, a 13th century rotunda with frescoes (16th cen., Renaissance) and a Holy Grave (1303). A winged altar (1524) stands in the northern side chapel next to the transept. It borders on the Choir of St. Thomas, from which a lovely Gothic staircase, the "Schnegg", leads upward to the upper Chapel of Saint Nicholas.

Between the Choir of St. Thomas and the crossing are the ornately carved choir stalls (15th cen.). The last chapel along the north aisle is the Gothic Welserkapelle (15th cen.).

The former **Jesuit Church** ⓫ (begun 1604, Rococo furnishings) is at the eastern end of the Münsterplatz, parallel to it is the one-time Jesuit Seminary (1609). Back then, the Jesuits were already performing plays here. The stage is still used by the city theatre today, making it nearly 400 years old and one of the oldest in Germany. At Münsterplatz there are two remarkable secular buildings: The Cathedral Hotel of St. John (originally a collegiate church starting in the 10th cen., present structure dates from 1889) and the house "Zur Kunkel" (No. 5, first-floor frescoes from 1300!). We continue to head toward the lake, then follow the wide Konzilstraße and turn onto Brückengasse, where we immediately find ourselves in front of the "Spitalkellerei" ("Spital Wine Cellar", ca. 1500). It is already part of the Niederburg district, the oldest in Constance, and manages the two vineyards in Constance and at Meersburg. Diagonally opposite is the former Zoffingen Monastery (1257) with its very with plain church. Now we follow Brückengasse and turn right twice right away, so that the Rheingasse first brings us to the Government Building, which was built in 1609 as a Cathedral Deanery. The Rheinstraße ends at the enormous **Rheintorturm** ⓬ ("Rhine Gate Tower" ca. 1400), which once guarded the wooden bridge over the Rhine. Part of the bridge that has survived is the figure of its patron saint, Nepomuk. Further along the banks of the Rhine, statutes of two Constance bishops and of the Baron Bertold von Zähringen and Baron Leopold von Baden were erected in the 19th century. Looking at these gives us something to pass the time as we near the **Powder Tower** ⓭, which once former the north-west corner of the city wall.

Constance, St. Mary's Cathedral: A view down the plain nave to the pulpit and the main altar.

Cathedral: The Holy Grave (ca. 1280). ▶

▼ *Constance, Cathedral: the Majestas-Goldscheibe (ca. 1000).*

Constance: The Rheintorturm once guarded the wooden bridge over the See-rhein. In the background is the spire of the cathedral.

On our way back, we stick to the course of the Seerhein and then the lakeshore. Thus right after passing by the Spital Wine Cellar and underneath the railway dike, we come to the **"Island" ⑭**. There was a Dominican monastery here from 1235 to 1785, in which various delegations conferred during the council. After the monastery was disbanded, the buildings were used for various purposes, including as a cotton factory and as a University; today the complex houses an island hotel. The former monastery church is now a hall in which the guest can behold the medieval murals. Re-crossing the bridge, we follow the course of the lakeshore through the city gardens and back to our starting point at the harbour. To the south of it we can see the "Klein-Venedig" quarter (Little Venice quarter), where since 1999 a

special attraction for the inhabitants of the town as well as for tourists has been created: the "Sea Life Constance". On an area of 3000 m2 the visitor can follow the Rhine making a wonderful journey from the Alps to the North Sea. More than 3000 fresh-water and salt-water fish "populate" the more than 30 aquariums together with other water animals: trouts, pikes, octopuses, rays, sharks and conger-eels. The visitor can admire the biggest of these water reservoirs (300000 l) and its "inhabitants" at close quarters through a tunnel; this way he has the impression of finding himself at the bottom of the sea.

In addition to the aquariums the plant

Constance: The joys of vacation on the terrace of the Insel-Hotel.

shows instructive representations of the Alps, the Lake Constance, the Rhine with a waterfall as well as reproductions of a port, a lock, a weir, the banks of a river and a shipwreck.

The same building is home to the only museum that deals with the natural history of Lake Constance. Here visitors will find all kinds of information and exhibits about the history of the lake. Topics covered run the gamut from primeval history to the latest knowledge about the biology of the water, pollution, and fishing. A separate department is devoted just to birds, especially those in the nearby Wollmatinger Marsh Wildlife Preserve.

On the other side of the Rhine bridge is the district of Petershausen, which is named after the Benedictine Abbey of Petershausen (10th cen. onward). Today the abbey buildings, which have since been restored, serve as a cultural centre, city archive, and branch of the State Museum of Archaeology. Above all, however, many of the leisure-time facilities that are part and parcel of a modern tourist spot are located in Petershausen: two outdoor pools and a thermal pool, a yachting harbour and a ship's landing, Kneipp cure facilities, a gambling casino, and the "Haus des Gastes" (Visitor Centre) in the exquisite art-nouveau villa "Prym", which was built for a snap-fastener manufacturer. From the Seestraße (lovely 19th cen. patrician houses) and the streets and paths leading off of it, one has a lovely view across the "Constance Funnel" the historic city centre of Constance and Kreuzlingen. Other scenic outlooks are on the Raiteberg (observation tower built 1912) and on the Gießberg on the campus of the university.

Of course a city like Constance, especially one blessed with the presence of a college and a university, also has a lot to offer in the cultural sector. Besides the historic buildings and the collections often housed within them, as well as the aforementioned city theatre, this especially means big events like the "Classics Live" concert series with the Southwest German Philharmonic Orchestra, the "Constance Fall Jazz Festival", the historic Fasnacht in the "fifth season" of the year, and the "Seenachtfest" held in Constance's sister city Kreuzlingen.

An unforgettable experience, the underwater tunnel of the new "Sea Life Constance" to walk through!

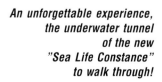

Mainau Island

It is only 7 km - crosswise over the tip of the Bodanrück Peninsula - from Constance to the famous scenic isle of Mainau, putting it within easy reach by bicycle, ship or city bus. The Staad district, which is half way between Constance and Mainau, is already situated on the Überlinger See and marks the point of departure for the ferry crossing to Meersburg (4.5 km, 20 minutes).

Subsequently we pass Konstanz-Allmannsdorf, a district of the city which, in the Lorettokapelle ("Loretto Chapel", 1638) and the St.-Georgs-Kirche ("Church of Saint George", 1745, master builder Anton Beer) still has at least two valuable historic buildings. The observation deck of the water tower offers a pleasant panorama, permitting, among other things, a sneak peak of Mainau Island.

From the mainland, one reaches the island via a dike and a bridge. Here we are greeted by the "Schwedenkreuz" ("Cross

An aerial view of the Island of Mainau, including the castle and parks.

Information

Blumeninsel Mainau GmbH, D-78465 Mainau Island, phone: 07531/303-0, fax 303-248, for guided tours ring 303-109, for dining information ring 303-156.
Mainau Blumenjahr: *Mid. March - October: Island, palms house and palace church 7 AM - 8 PM, butterfly house 10 AM - 8 PM, art exhibits 11 AM - 7 PM, "Lichtblicke im Gärtnerturm" 10 AM - 5 PM.* ***Mainau Fall and Winter:*** *November - Mid. March: Island, palms house and palace church 9 AM - 6 PM, butterfly house 11 AM - 5 PM, art exhibits 11 AM - 6 PM, "Lichtblicke im Gärtnerturm" 10 AM - 5 PM.*
Island bus: *between the mainland entrance and the Schwedenschenke. Mid. March - April and October 10:00 AM - 5:00 PM, May - September 9:00 AM - 6:00 PM.*

of the Swedes"), an over 400 year-old bronze crucifixion group. It probably stood next to the Palace Church until the Thirty Years' War, when it was taken away by the Swedish soldiers. Apparently, however, it soon proved too heavy for them to carry, so they simply sank the artwork in the lake where it still stands unscathed today.

The island was already owned by Reichenau Abbey in the 8th century; in 1272, it was donated to the Teutonic Order of Knights. Upon confiscation of church property in the Napoleonic era, the island was annexed to the Grand Duchy of Baden in 1806. Grand Duke Friedrich I. of Baden bought the island in 1853 and used it as a summer residence from 1857 until his death (1907). He had a park created and planted with many varieties of tropical trees, most of which he had brought home from his travels abroad. Since 1932, the property has belonged to Duke Lennart Bernadotte or the foundation named after him (since 1974), his consort, Countess Sonja, is the managing director of the foundation. The Duke, who is related to the Swedish Royal Family, has the 45 ha island (which rests upon molasse rock) turned into a "ship of flowers". Year after year, the island draws some 1.7 million

Mainau: The family of Count Lennart Bernadotte and his wife, Countess Sonja.

visitors. The foundation uses the proceeds from the parking and entrance fees not only to finance the gardens and the maintenance of the historic buildings, but is also committed to sciences (annual meeting of Nobel Prize winners), conservation, and protection of the environment and historical monuments.

After passing the ticket window, first fol-

A bird's-eye-view of Mainau Palace; the Palace Church of St. Marien is at right.

Mainau: A view across the well-groomed flower beds to the Palace Church.

low the lakeshore to the right. This takes us past the restaurant "Lauenstüble", a playground, a small animal enclosure, a goldfish pond, and a sculpture. The "Wild Rose and Rosebush Path" runs parallel to this above. It is worth strolling along, especially during the main blossom time in May/ June, when it is surpassed only by the "Italian rose garden" south of the palace-complex. Its terrace affords visitors a wonderful view. The palace and the church were built more 250 years ago under the direction of Giovanni Gaspare Bagnato, whose grave is in the crypt of the church. The stucco work and altars by artist Joseph Anton Feuchtmayer are also worth a look. The palace gable bears a large coat-of-arms of the Teutonic Order that had the building constructed.

To the northeast, the harbour breakwaters and the piers look like fingers stretching toward the opposite shore. Between the palace and the harbour is the restaurant "Comtureykeller", in which visitors can see a historic Zehntfaß

(1689), a cask with a capacity of 25,000 l. To the east, well-tended park paths lead past a defensive tower to the Pfauenwiese and the arboretum with its stately, exotic park trees (including giant trees), all of which are well marked. Especially from Panoramaweg - between Mediterranterrasse and Großherzog-Friedrich-Terrasse - visitors have a magnificent view southward, topped only by the view from the last of the terraces mentioned. Nearby are the small hothouses in which 6000 types of orchids - 1500 of them wild - unfold their magnificent blossoms. From mid-March until May, they are the focus of the Grand Orchid Show in the Palmengarten. In the "Mainau blooming calendar", they are followed starting in April by the early-blooming narcissuses, tulips, and hyacinths (800 varieties), azaleas and rhododendrons (nearly 300 varieties) in May, 300,000 sunflowers and 30,000 rose trees (election of the "Rose Queen") in June, and, as a finale, some 20,000 dahlias of more than 200 varieties,

*Mainau Island:
A magnificent cascade
of flowers.*

the loveliest of which is elected "Queen of the Dahlias" each year by the public. Besides these, the fruit-bearing banana trees, palms, orange, mandarine, and lemon trees receive a great deal of attention during the summer months and are proof of the mild climate prevailing on the island. The citrus show (starting in 1997) exhibits 55 varieties of the sub-tropic "golden apples", a collection that is unique in Europe. Since 1996, visitors can also attend outdoor concerts of classical music.

Thanks to many facilities and institutions that do not depend on the seasons, the island remains attractive even in fall and winter. The largest butterfly house in Germany was dedicated here in 1996. Visitors can experience up to 20 tropical species of butterflys, often a hundred or more fluttering around at a time, surrounded by a jungle landscape in full bloom. Under the motto "Lichtblick im Gärtnerturm" the old defensive tower was turned into an information centre about "Nature and Culture in the Lake Constance Region". With the help of an elborate 3D slide show, among other things, the program at the center extols the beauty of the Lake Constance landscape and urges that it be protected. A winter garden exhibit offers tips on redesigning one's own home. A special "Mainau Fall and Winter" program offers classical concerts, readings, and top-calibre exhibitions in a very wide variety of artistic styles, as well as gardening seminars and gourmet cooking classes. In this way, the "flowering Isle of Mainau" has advanced, almost on the side, to become an important regional cultural centre.

Mainau: An exotic butterfly.

On the Bodanrück

Litzelstetten, Dingelsdorf and Wallhausen are situated to the north-west of the island Mainau. These three towns on the Überlinger See were incorporated into the city of Constance in the 1970's. The peaceful climatic health resort of Litzelstetten has a parish church (19th cent.) with Rococo pews as well as a beach and camping grounds. It is an excellent starting point for hikes on the Bodanrück. To the north, in the direction of Fliesshorn, there is a wildlife preservation area. From the hilltop and flat slope of the Purren (508 m), there is a nice view of the Mainau Island out over the Überlinger See over to Birnau Abbey Church and the Obersee. The Oberdorf district of Constance-Dingelsfdorf is located two kilometres away. The Teutonic Order of Knights had the harmonious Holy Cross Chapel built in 1747. The architect of this Rococo-style gem was - as was the case on Mainau - Giovanni G. Bagnato. The creators of the varied stucco work (Pozzi) and the ceiling frescoes (Appiani) were also involved in the

View out over the Überlinger See of the resort town of Constance-Dingelsdorf at the foot of the wooded Bodanrück.

Dettingen-Wallhausen: *Tourist Office, phone: 07533/1744, fax: 730*
Dingelsdorf: *Tourist Association, City Hall, phone: 07533/5750*
Litzelstetten: *Tourist Office, City Hall, phone: 07531/44062*

construction of the palace on the island. In the main town, the former fishing village of Dingelsdorf, the main attractions are the enormous half-timbered structures (17th/18th cent.) in the centre of town, probably the most beautiful in the whole Lake Constance region. The Gothic parish church of St. Nicholas (1493) with its Baroque furnishings is also worth seeing. Beach lovers, however, will probably like the sprawling, level beach most of all. It is ideal for small children and non-swimmers.

From here, it is another two km to Constance-Wallhausen and the inviting beach there. This fishing village, more than 800 years old, has evolved into a renowned beach resort with a water sports centre in recent years. The flat beach ends just to the north-west of Wallhausen. The hills of the Bodanrück slope down to the lake even steeper here. This is especially apparent at the Marienschlucht (i.e. "Mary's Gorge"), which can be reached by foot in about 45 minutes. On the way there, you pass by the ruins of Burghof, located on the lake. It takes less time to drive the car via Dettingen (St. Verena church with lovely Rococo pulpit) and Langenrain to the ruins of Kargegg. From the parking lot there, it is just a few metres to the start of the enchanting gorge. Visitors have a great view out over the lake from here. The gorge itself is only 100 m long, but 65 m deep. The walls of the rock covered with moss and lichens are only one meter apart in some places and hikers literally have to squirm their way between them. In compensation for the strenuous trek over wooden steps and planks, they are rewarded occasionally with a view of the sparkling surface of the lake. In the lower portion of the gorge, before the murmuring brook empties into the lake, hikers get the feeling of being in a miniature fjord. The gorge, narrowly cut into the sandstone of the Bodanrück, is a wildlife preservation area and can also be reached in the summertime via excursion ship from Überlingen, Bodman and Sipplingen.

A romantic footpath leads through the rugged Marienschlucht down to the lake.

Bodman-Ludwigshafen

From Langenrain, we keep to the right and, via Liggeringen, reach the town of Bodman on the south shore of the lake after about 10 km. Although it only has a population of about 1200 at present, the town is one of the oldest in the entire Lake Constance region. Artefacts from the Stone and Bronze Age bear witness to a prehistoric settlement. A document from the year 890 exists which calls the lake "lacus potmanicus", after the town that is presently called Bodman. The Carolingians maintained an imperial palace here, and castles were built on the surrounding mountaintops. In 1277, the Lords of Bodman gained possession of the former palatinate and the town. The parish church (17th cent.) with its striking Gothic spire is built on a Carolingian foundation. The palace of the count is located in the sprawling park. It is a four-wing complex from the 18th century in Biedermeier style. The building is the residence and administrative seat of the family of the Count of Bodman and not open to the public. The park can be visited on working days from April 1 to October 31. The massive building of the Weintorkel (1772) also belonged to the count. It bears witness to the centuries-old winegrowing tradition of the lord of the castle and the locals. The half-timbered structure with the enormous hipped roof presently serves in part as a wine bar and also occasionally holds exhibitions of the works of well-known artists from the region.

Aside from that, the town has other sights to offer visitors, for example, the gatehouse and the museum in the city hall. Mainly, though, visitors come here for peace and quiet away from the main thoroughfares and for the countless hiking trails in the area of the Bodanrück, e.g. trails to the ruins of Altbodman (excellent vantage points), to the top of the Frauenberg (former castle, later abbey, pilgrimage chapel since 1309, church services for pilgrims), to the bison enclosure or to the wildlife preservation area of Aachried between Bodman and Ludwigshafen. You can even join a guided tour of this absolutely beautiful, expansive area. It is a valuable refuge for brooding birds such as little grebes, nightingales and kingfishers as well as for thousands of migrating birds that spend the winter here or rest here during their long treks. Therefore, nature lovers constantly come across exciting opportunities for observation and picture taking both from the lakeshore path and the platform. The bordering wild orchards also serve as a refuge for rare and endangered species of birds and plants.

Bodman's partner town, Ludwigshafen (pop. 2500), is located opposite Bodman. It is easy to reach and situated in a charming countryside surrounded by fruit orchards and at the foot of wooded hills. Visitors have a magnificent view over the town and out over the lake to Bodman from the edge of the forest: you can even see the Alps from here on clear days. The town first appeared in a

Tourist Office, Hafenstrasse 5, D-78351 Bodman-Ludwigshafen,
Phone: 07773/930040, fax: 930043
Bodman Museum: *April - Sept., Monday - Thursday 9 AM - 12 noon and 2 PM - 4 PM, Oct. - March, Monday - Friday 9 AM - 12 noon, for group reservations ring 07773/939695.*

Information

Bodman-Ludwigshafen: the palace gardens of Bodman in front of the parish church.

document as "Sernatingen" in 1145. It belonged to Austria for centuries before being annexed to the Grand Duchy of Baden at the beginning of the 19th century. The spacious harbour was dedicated in 1826 and named after Grand Duke Ludwig. The entire municipality then adopted this name - by order of the municipal council. The transport and customs harbour did a great deal of business until the transport of goods was transferred to the railroad at the end of the 19th century. The enormous customs house is a remnant of its short-lived heyday as a place of trade.

Situated in the middle of the sprawling park directly on the lake, this stately structure now serves as a civic and visitors' centre for conferences, seminars and numerous social and cultural events. In this way, the former Grand Ducal Principal Customs House of Baden, with a large-capacity restaurant, has become a landmark and social meeting point of the small resort town, which also offers a beach and a sailing school.

Bodman: old gatehouse.

Sipplingen

The romantic resort town of Sipplingen is situated on a very narrow strip of land on the shore, facing the midday sun, between Ludwigshafen and Überlingen. Despite the favourable climate here, winegrowing has been mostly replaced by fruit growing. In the spring, the settlement is enveloped in blossoming cherry trees below the wooded hills, while its most precious product,

kirsch, can be enjoyed all year round. Beautifully renovated half-timbered houses, decorated with flowers and charming front gardens, accent the small-town grace especially in the centre of town and brought Sipplingen first place in the national contest "Making Our Village Even More Beautiful". Fishermen settled in the protected location on the lake in pile dwell-

Sipplingen: town centre with boat harbour on the Überlinger See. On the opposite side: Bodman and the wooded Bodanrück mountain chain.

Tourist Office (Haus des Gastes), D-78354 Sipplingen,
Phone: 07551/8096-29, Fax: 3570
Sipplingen Adventure World: Middle of March to beginning of Nov., daily 10:00 AM - 6:00 PM, Christmas racation daily 11:00 AM - 5:00 PM, other seasons Saturday, Sunday, holidays 11:00 AM- 5:00 PM.
For more information: phone: 07551/915653, fax: 91654.

Sipplingen: Fountain and half-timbered house on Rathausplatz.

ings as far back as the early Stone Age. Later, fortified castles towered over the town. The ruins of these castles can still be viewed today, as can the finds from prehistoric times. Some of these are in the former train station, while others are on display in the Überlingen Museum of Local History and in the Unteruhldingen Pile Dwelling Museum.

Valuable buildings in town include the half-timbered structure of the Bruderschafts-shaus (i.e. "House of Brotherhood", after 1600) and the five-story Konstanzer Spi-talhof (i.e. "Constance Hospital Court"), especially recognisable by its typical stag-gered gables. In the city hall (17th cent.), the Bürgersaal (i.e. "Citizens' Hall") with its coffered ceiling is particularly notewor-thy. The Gothic parish church has a Ba-roque interior with the patron saints, St. Martin and St. George, both works by art-ist Joseph Anton Feuchtmayer, and a

Madonna statue (17th cent.). There are many more treasures from times past for curious visitors to discover, especially in the centre of town with its little squares and narrow lanes and paths.

On the other hand, the lovely lakeshore facilities, including a beach, boat rental and the two boat harbours, where guest slips are always available, are contemporary in style. Besides water sports, you can also spend an active holiday here playing min-iature golf, boccie, chess and tennis. Those who prefer more tranquillity can go to the Sipplingen landing dock as a starting point for boat excursions on the lake, maybe even a romantic moonlight cruise accompanied by music and candlelight.

Above the lakeshore, the street called "In der Breite" leads up the hill to the "Erleb-niswelt Sipplingen" (i.e. "Sipplingen Ad-venture World") spread out over 1600 m². This is the largest model car collection in

Sipplingen: "Erlebniswelt".

Sipplingen: A view, across one of the boat harbours, of the town centre around the Gothic parish church of Sts. Martin and George.

the world with more than 20,000 models of automobiles from 40 countries, including original antique cars and technical devices from the time of the respective vehicles. Other rooms in the Erlebniswelt include exhibits of model trains, a doll and "Steiff" stuffed animal museum, a video room as well as a model shop and a museum café. There is also an adjacent reptile exhibit with about 100 animals; snakes and lizards as well as spiders and scorpions.

Thanks to its location on the slopes of a mountain, Sipplingen is also ideal for hiking in the surroundings (40 km of marked trails). Inviting benches lure hikers to sit a while and take in the view of the town and lake. An instructional geological trail provides information on the origins of the landscape. Thanks to the location on the slopes facing the south, many rare plants thrive here, in particular species of wild orchids which are usually prefer a Mediterranean climate. After a half-hour's march up the mountain, hikers reach the ruins of Alt-Hohenfels Castle, where the Minnesinger Burkhard von Hohenfels lived in the 13th century. Continuing on, hikers arrive at the Haldenhof. It once served as a hospital court and belonged to the im-

perial city of Überlingen. Today, it is a resort restaurant where visitors can enjoy a magnificent view.

Atop nearby Sipplinger Berg (701 m) is an important part of a marvel of modern technology, the "Quelltopf" (i.e., springhead) and the treatment plant for the Lake Constance water supply. The water is taken from Lake Constance to the east of Sipplingen at a depth of 60 m (temp. around 5°C) and then conveyed onto the mountain by means of giant pumps. The water is filtered multiple times in the plant and disinfected through the addition of ozone. About 3.5 million people in Baden-Württemberg are supplied with this drinking water: via Stuttgart and Heilbronn all the way to Bad Mergentheim and Heidelberg. On average, 4100 l per second are taken from the lake, which is approximately the same as the evaporation factor on the surface or 1.1% of the total water quantity which empties out of the Obersee as the Seerhein by Constance. As a side note, along its way to North Baden, the new main pipeline 2 (2.25 m diameter) crosses the Swabian Highlands in a tunnel that winds through the mountains at a depth of up to 260 m and for a distance of 24 km.

Water treatment plant on Sipplinger Berg.

Überlingen

A highway with a scenic view of the lake leads in the direction of Überlingen. However, we turn off of the highway already at the town district of Goldbach, a picturesque place tucked away between vineyards. Its early Romanesque Chapel of St. Sylvester dates back to ca. 1000 and has remnants of medieval mural paintings that are worth seeing. Just a few hundred meters to the north, visitors can marvel at a "Gletschermühle" (i.e. "Glacier Mill") from a vantage point. This is a glacial hole carved out of the molasse rock during the last Ice Age. There is a nice view of the lake from Eglisbohl, a hill east of Goldbach.

Leaving Goldbach, we reach the centre of Überlingen in just a few minutes. This town was mentioned for the first time in

Überlingen: early Romanesque chapel of St. Sylvester in the town district of Goldbach.

Information

Kur- und Touristik Überlingen GmbH ("Health Resort and Tourist Office of Überlingen"), Landungsplatz 14, D-88662 Überlingen, phone: 07551/9911-22, fax: 9911-35
Museum of Local History:
Tuesday - Saturday 9:00 AM - 12:30 PM + 2:00 - 5:00 PM, Sunday and holidays 10:00 AM -3:00 PM. Closed Tuesday if Monday is a holiday. November - March, closed Sunday and holidays.
Historic Zeughaus:
May - September Tuesday-Friday 10:30 AM - 12:00 AM.

a document in 770 as the royal corvée court of "Iburinga". The name translates as the "home of the boar". The ending "-inga", presently written as "-lingen" is typical of Alemannic settlements of that time. Kaiser Friedrich I Barbarossa granted it a city charter in the 12th century. It later became a free imperial city and at-

city fortifications date back to this time. The Thirty Years' War (1618-1648) brought an end to the prosperous times, as it did with so many other cities in Southern Germany. Thanks to its mineral spring, which was well-known as far back as 1474, the city was able to establish a reputation as a health resort early

Überlingen: view of the old town, with the historical buildings bunched up around the Cathedral of St. Nicholas.

tained modest prosperity by trading corn, wine and salt. Most of the significant structures such as the cathedral, the city hall, numerous patrician houses and the

on, thereby soothing the economic downturn. Although Überlingen lost its imperial freedom and was annexed to Baden in 1802, attractive bathing facilities, promenades, parks and hotels were constructed in the middle of the 19th century. Nobility, the upper middle class and artists visited the town, which became known as "Little Nice on Lake Constance". Its prominent guests included the Queen of Württemberg, the Margrave of Baden as well as the poets Ludwig Uhland, Gustav Schwab and their colleague Annette von Droste-Hülshoff. When the curative powers of the spring weakened at the end of the century, the town succeeded in drawing the attention of its visitors to the charming old town, the scenic location on the lake and the southern flair. After World War II, it began the construction of fasting clinics and Kneipp facilities, receiving state approval as a Kneipp health resort in 1956 - the southern-most in Germany and the only one in Baden-Württemberg, by the way. Today, Überlingen is frequently visited health resort and place to spend a holiday, as well as the cultural centre of Linzgau and a stop along the Upper Swabian Baroque Road.

Überlingen's old town is roughly in the form of a triangle, with the lakeshore at its base. We begin our walking tour about in the middle of this base line, at the ships landing. The landing is dominated by the striking Greth building, the former warehouse. Today the Tourist Information Office, a cinema, and a market hall with a restaurant and café are located here. The town replaced the former lakeshore fortifications with one of the most sprawling lake promenades with room for beaches, harbour facilities for yachts and sporting boats, sailing and windsurfing schools, health resort and sport facilities as well as campgrounds.

In 1999, an unusual fountain by Bodman-based sculptor Peter Lenk, whose works already caused a furore in Constance years ago, was dedicated in front of the Greth Building. The basin of the fountain, which is populated mainly by older water-nymphs, is crowned by the legendary "Rider of Lake Constance", immortalised by poet Gustav Schwab in a 19th century ballad. The historic rider crossed the lake from Dingelsdorf to here during the "Seegfrörne" of 1573, leaving the already thawing ice with not a moment to spare.

East of the Greth House in Hafenstrasse, there are also two town residences of cloisters from the area; the Walderhof (Wald Abbey) and Petershauserhof (16th cent. Petershausen Abbey in Constance). The wide street opposite the Greth House, known as "Hofstatt" today, was the fish market at one time. The town gallery "Fauler Pelz" (i.e. "Lazy Bones") and the late Gothic Zeughaus (i.e. "Arsenal"), presently housing a weaponry museum, are located in the house block to the west of that.

The city hall (14th century and later) stands at the northern end of the Hofstatt. Its east wing was built at the end of the 15th century in the style of Florentine Renaissance buildings. The Cathedral of St. Nicholas is situated to the north-west of the city hall across an empty square. The south tower was constructed back in the first part of the 15th century and fitted with the almost 9 tonne Osanna bell.

Although construction of the church lasted until 1586, the builders neglected to follow through on plans to build the tower up to the height of its northern neighbour (78 m), which bears the remaining 7 bells of the impressive peal. The Mount of Olives ensemble at the south-west corner was created in 1495. The interior of the church was also left primarily in the original late Gothic style, probably because renovation exceeded the financial means of the population. The high altar is by for the most valuable piece among the furnishings. It was made by Jörg Zürn in co-operation with his three brothers

Überlingen: the warf is dominated by the restored Greth building, a former warehouse.

Überlingen: since 1999 the „Horseman of the Lake of Constance" by the Bodman sculptor Peter Lenk is the subject of many discussions.

and his father around 1613. The four fili-gree-carved statue ensembles made of linden wood portray the Annunciation, the Birth of Christ, the Coronation of Mary and the Crucifixion. The masterpiece with many statues is 10 m high and is protected by an artistically fashioned Rococo lattice (18th cen.). The tabernacle, another work by Jörg Zürn, is located to the side at the level of the altar. His family belonged to the Überlingen Fishers' Guild, whose patron saint was also the patron saint of the church, namely St. Nicholas. The choir seats from 1430 are also located behind the choir lattice. The 13 side altars of the nave date back to the 15th century and later. Two of these in the south side aisles come from the workshop of the Zürn family.

On Münsterplatz, attentive visitors can see a large coat of arms of the town on the gable of the former town office (presently town archives), to which the handsome portal belongs. From here, we proceed up the Krummebergstrasse which leads us to one of the loveliest patrician courts of all, the Reichlin-von-Mel-

deggsches Haus. Like the east wing of the city hall, it was built in the 15th century in rusticated dressed ashlar, completely in Italian Renaissance style. The town purchased the representative building in 1908 and set up a museum of local history there. The main sights to see here are the stuccoed hall from 1695 (Schmuzer), the house chapel (1486) and the terrace garden, which affords a beautiful view out over the roofs of the old town. Its exhibits include quality sculptures, incl. three sculptures from the most significant Baroque artists on Lake Constance, Joseph Anton Feuchtmayer. The old doll rooms and a Torkel (i.e. "winepress") from 1697 from Hagnau are also of note.

The town moat was located just a few steps away. The towers "Rosenobel", right close by and, to the south-west, St. Johann's Tower (both 17th cen.) are the only remnants of this.

Going back through the Krummebergstrasse and turning right immediately, we come to Wiestorstrasse, which we follow down to the Franziskanertor (i.e. "Franciscan Gate"). Tradition has it that the patrician house "Gunzoburg" to the west is situated at the place where the ancestral castle of the Alemannic Duke Gunzo once stood around the year 600. The gate tower signifies the beginning of the cloister district of the Franciscans, whose main structure (built in the 18th century) now serves as a home for the aged. The focal point of spiritual life, however, was the late Gothic Franciscan church (14th/15th cent.), the interior of which was modified in the Baroque period. Joseph Anton Feuchtmayer created the high altar and some of the quality statues and was even responsible for the stucco work accompanying the frescoes from Franz Ludwig Herrmann.

From the gate, we proceed along Aufkircher Strasse towards the north-west and pass by the simple late-Gothic

Jodak Chapel (frescoes from the 15th-17th cent. worth seeing), before coming upon another gate tower of the town fortifications, the Aufkircher Tor. From this point on, we walk in the direction of Lake Constance along the former town moat, which cuts through the upper park grounds of the town gardens in this area. Visitors can revel in a deer enclosure and lovely greens with subtropical plants, beds of roses and the noteworthy cactus ensemble (80-90 species, the largest open-air cactus complex in Germany). The "Quellturm" (i.e. "Spring Tower") is at the west end of the town gardens above the spring, which was once acclaimed for its curative powers. The Kurmittelhaus (i.e. "Spa Centre") is located at the south-east corner, below the Gallerturm. Finally, Bahnhofstrasse separates the town gardens from the spa gardens with its various facilities; the spa hall, the spa complex, the "Haus des Kurgastes" and the "Schweigewiese".

From the Cristophstrasse - an eastern extension of Bahnhofstrasse - we turn left once more onto Grabenstrasse, then right onto Steinhausgasse. This is the location of another cloister residence, the Salmansweilerhof (1535) of the Cistercian abbey of Salem. The Steinhaus (16th cent.), which gave the street its name, is just opposite. The spital wine cellar is now housed behind its corbie-step gable façade. The lane intersects with Franziskanerstrasse, which is marked by a few very lovely gable houses from the 16th century, many decorated with small oriels. From here, we proceed along the shortest way back via Marktstrasse to the beach on Lake Constance with the landing.

In addition to the cultural events already mentioned, there are, of course, also health resort concerts and the famous Alemannic Mardi Gras. Since the Thirty

Überlingen: Ornately wrought cantilevers on an inn.

Years' War, there is a procession twice a year (in May and June) through Überlingen. The silver Madonna sculpture is always part of the procession. It is said to have protected the town from being captured and plundered by the Swedish mercenaries in the spring of 1634. The participants in this procession wear festive garments: the women and girls often wear the traditional Überlingen dress. After the second procession each year, local boys thrill spectators with the "Schwertletanz" (i.e. "Little Swords' Dance"), thereby graphically reviving a part of the past.

The territory of the town of Überlingen stretches from the level of Lake Constance (395 m above mean sea level) up to 650 m and is criss-crossed with horse, bicycle and hiking trails (more than 70 km). An instructional geological trail and an exercise trail provide more incentives for the mind and body. If you're into small balls, the town has miniature golf, boccie, and tennis - outdoor and indoor - as well as a nicely situated golf course.

Birnau Abbey

Überlingen's town districts extend primarily from the shore of Lake Constance upwards, surrounded by orchards, vineyards and woods. The former fishing village of Nussdorf is of particular note. It is situated on Lake Constance east of the centre of town. It has a wide range of inns, bed and breakfast houses, and campgrounds as well as a beach, which have impressively

The Baroque abbey church of Birnau in the midst of vineyards, one of the trademarks of Lake Constance.

Information

Birnau Abbey, Birnau-Maurach 4, D-88690 Uhldingen-Mühlhofen, phone 07556/92030
Hours of opening: Summer 7:00 AM - 7:00 PM, winter 8:00 AM - 5:30 PM. Tours by appointment: reservations by letter or telephone required.

established it among the ranks of the rural resorts on the lake. The street names of the town give visitors a short lesson in Lake Constance fish species, starting at A for Alet and Äsche (i.e. "alet" and "grayling ") all the way to Z for Zander (i.e. "lake perch"). The Nussdorf Chapel is worth visiting. It contains a carved altar from the 15th century and frescoes from the 16th century. The famous pilgrimage church of Birnau lies close to the town limits of Nussdorf on a hill with a panorama view in the middle of vineyards. It is a highlight along the Upper Swabian Baroque Road. The previous structure "Alt-Birnau" was about 3 km further to the north-west and was also a filial abbey of the Cistercian Abbey of Salem, just as the present-day "Neu-Birnau". The famous architect Peter Thumb built the church starting in 1746. It forms a harmonic unit in connection with the provost buildings - to either side of the tower. In this way, the Salem Abbey, in keeping with the trend of the times, joined in the competition for the most beautiful buildings and used it as a summer residence for its abbots. In 1803, Birnau Abbey along with all other ecclesiastical German possessions was turned over to secular hands. However, in 1919, Prince Max of Baden left it over to the Cistercians of Mehrerau by Bregenz. They tend to the buildings here and in Maurach - on the lakeshore below - to this day.

As is the case with all Baroque structures, the beauty of the overall work is revealed to visitors primarily through the lavishly decorated interior flooded with light, whose powerful pilasters leave much room for large windows and ceiling frescoes. The Augsburg court painter Gottfried Bernhard Göz created the main fresco "Verherrlichung der lieblichen Mutter" (i.e. "Glorification of the Sweet Virgin Mother") mainly in brown tones and numerous other ceiling frescoes. The rather reserved stucco work comes from Joseph Anton Feuchtmayer, who also designed the seven altars and the countless angels and statues of saints. Among the angels floating above, the original "Honigschlecker" (i.e. "Honey Gourmet") at the altar of Saint Bernhard of Clairvaux to the right where the altar meets the choir is the most interesting to behold. The main altar with charming angels playing on its baldachin was modified much later. Beneath that, we see the miracle-working image of the "Liebliche Mutter von Birnau" (i.e. "Sweet Virgin Mother of Birnau"), a work from the 15th century. The Oberhof Winery is opposite the church in the direction of the mountain. It belongs to the Margraves of Baden. Curious visitors can join in an expertly narrated wine tasting by appointment or witness the traditional Uhldingen Wine Festival here at the end of October.

Birnau Abbey Church: "Der Honigschlecker", putto by J.A. Feuchtmayer.

Birnau Abbey Church: magnificently furnished Baroque pilgrimage church of the Cistercians with paintings by Gottfried Bernhard Göz as well as stucco

work and altars by Joseph Anton Feuchtmayer.

Uhldingen-Mühlhofen

From Birnau, hikers can easily get to Unteruhldingen on a pleasant footpath, too. On the way, you pass by the hamlet of Seefelden, which is among the oldest parishes in the Lake Constance region. Tradition has it that St. Gall held a mass here around 630, and there was a convent her in the late Middle Ages. The Romanesque tower from this period on the otherwise late Gothic parish church is still standing. Between Seefelden and Unteruhldingen, the footpath crosses the interesting nature conservation are of "Seefelder Aach", another path along the stream leads to Oberuhldingen. The train station, the city hall, and the library as well as tennis courts and a skateboard track are located in this town district. The

Unteruhldingen: Reconstruction of dwellings from the early Stone Age in the Pile Dwelling Museum. In the background is the pilgrimage church of Birnau.

Fremdenverkehrbetriebe GmbH (Tourist Office), Schulstrasse 12, D-88690 Uhldingen-Mühlhofen, phone: 07556/9216-0, fax: 9216-20
Pfahlbaumuseum: April - September daily 8:00 AM- 6:00 PM, October daily 9:00 AM- 5:00 PM, March and November weekends + holidays 9:00 AM - 5:00 PM, Dec., Jan., Feb., Sunday 10:00 AM - 4:00 PM, guided tours on workdays by arrangement. For appointments and more information: ring 07556/8543.

Pile Dwelling Museum of Unteruhldingen: see the pile dwellings furnished almost entirely as they were back then.

executioner's axe in the coat of arms of the town dates back to the time previous to 1264 when the town was still in the possession of the Lords of Oberrieden who then transferred possession to the Salem Abbey.

The town district of Unteruhldingen lies directly on the lake. Today, it is most famous for its Pile Dwelling Museum. In the Middle Ages, the town was so well-known as a harbour along the way to the royal city of Constance that Kaiser Friedrich "Barbarossa" himself regulated the controversial shipping traffic by decree. Both regularly scheduled and chartered excursion ships put to shore here to this day during the summer season. A definite tourist community is waiting to greet visitors here, a far cry from the times of fishers and ship captains. There is a tourist office in the visitors' centre prepared to answer all your questions pertaining to recreational activities. The centre also has rooms exhibitions, evening music, and theatre performances where you can go to enjoy an afternoon coffee party and dance. Furthermore, there is an attractive beach (indoor pool in the town district of Mühlhofen), numerous excursion opportunities (many guided), various kinds of restaurants and numerous special events; such as Sunday promenade concerts, visitor greeting events, beach and barbecue parties, the wine festival and the Great Harbour Festival with the famous "Schrottregatta" (i.e. "Junk Regatta"), where the most original floating vehicle to make it to the finish line wins the contest. Pedestrians have the right of way throughout everywhere in town: motorists should leave their vehicles at the large parking lot outside of town. They are then transported to the harbour by means of the "Kurbähnle" (i.e. "little health resort train"), helping to reduce the amount of pollutants in the air. This mini-train is part of the environmentally

Pile Dwelling Museum: kitchen furnishings of early humans, reconstructed based primarily on finds from the Lake Constance region.

friendly tourism concept to which the community has devoted itself and which has brought it three related awards in a short period of time.

However, most visitors come to Unteruhldingen to see the world-famous pile dwellings. The Swiss archaeologist Ferdinand Keller discovered agglomerations of piles in Lake Zurich during low water back in 1854. The first reconstruction of two settlements from the early Stone Age and the Bronze Age were built starting in 1922 according to sketches and

excavation results on Lake Constance, in the upper Swabian Federseemoor as well as on the Swiss lakes at the foothills of the Alps.

In the impressive open-air museum, visitors can see how well the wooden constructions and tools, the clay vessels, weapons and stone tools, children's toys, jewellery and even remnants of clothing and food kept over the millennia. The newly constructed museum building on the mainland contains a clear presentation, especially of finds from Unter-

Family Games at the Pile Dwelling Museum: baking bread.

uhldingen and Sipplingen. The seminar rooms, archive and library of the adjacent Institute for Prehistory and Ancient History also serve the purposes of curious guests and researchers.

A guided tour lasting about 45 minutes first takes visitors to the village from the early Stone Age from about 5500 years ago. They get to see up close and impressively how our ancestors worked stone and wood, produced clay pots and materials, cooked, baked, hunted, fished and cultivated and harvested their fields. The progress on up to the Bronze Age - approximately 3000 years ago - is obvious in all of these techniques. Domestication of animals (cattle, pigs, sheep, goats) and metalworking including the manufacture of jewellery joined the range of capabilities. Even though it has been scientifically proven that the pile dwellings did not stand above water but rather in the marshy shores, they do provide an impressive, scientifically sound image of the living communities of that time.

Evening descends upon the Pile Dwelling Museum.

Salem and Heiligenberg

On our way from Oberuhldingen to Salem, we pass "Affenberg" (i.e. "Ape Mountain") after 3 km. More than 200 mountain apes, native to North Africa, live in the 20 ha open-air enclosure Along the 600 m circular path, visitors can watch the apes quietly and then view the ape museum afterwards, where they can see how Europeans and people from other cultures view their next of kin in the animal kingdom. A pond near the entrance is home to the "Storchenweiher" ("Stork Pond") with waterfowl and an impressive breeding colony of free-flying storks. The idyllic Tavern on "Ape Mountain" is located in Mendlishauser Hof, a former domain of Salem Abbey. It is located on "Prälatenweg" (i.e., "Prekate's Way"), halfway between the pilgrimage church at Birnau and this former abbey.

Another 4 km down the road, we reach the famous Salem Abbey, the most important location of the Cistercians in the

"Ape Mountain" in Salem: Barbary ape.

"Ape Mountain" in Salem: Stork.

Information

Salemer Kultur & Freizeit GmbH ("Salem Culture and Recreation Office"), Schloss Salem, D-88682 Salem
Hours: April through October weekdays 9:30 AM - 6:00 PM, Sunday and holidays 10:30 AM - 6:00 PM. Information Phone: 07553/81437, Fax: 8519, wine tasting Phone 81271.
Affenberg ("Ape Mountain"), D-88682 Salem Hours: *March 15 - November 1 daily 9:00 AM - 6:00 PMPhone: 07553/381, Fax: 6454.*
Tourist Office, D-88633 Heiligenberg, Phone 07554/99830, Fax: 998329.
Schloss der Fürsten zu Fürstenberg ("Palace of the Princes of Fürstenberg"):
April - October daily 9:00 AM - 11:30 AM + 1 - 5:00 PM, closed July 1 - August 15.

Salem Abbey: lower gate and - in the background - the Marstallbau, both works by the Baroque master builder Bagnato.

Middle Ages in South Germany as well as the most influential abbey in the Lake Constance region after the one in St. Gallen and on Reichenau Island.

It was founded in 1134 under the name of Salmannsweiler and renamed soon thereafter following the biblical Salem and Jeru-Salem. It prospered with the trade of wine, grains and salt and established trading offices in 29 cities. Between 1487 and its dissolution in 1803, Salem was an immediate abbey, only beholden to the Kaiser himself. Through expert guided tours, visitors can experience the architecture, art and history from 7 centuries from Gothic and Renaissance through Baroque and Rococo up to early classicism, which matured to new levels in the furnishings of the Gothic cathedral. The extraordinary alabaster furnishings come from the sculptor Johann Georg Dirr and his son-in-law J.G. Wieland. Besides countless vases, puttos and monuments, there are 27 altars adorning the church interior, bearing witness to the self-confidence and need for representation of the abbey in the 18th century.

The sprawling wings of the former convent building are grouped around three inner courtyards. The Margrave of Baden uses some of the rooms as living quarters. The other rooms furnished in lavish Baroque style serve as a museum

Salem: side aisle of the gothic cathedral.

Abbey Salem: the fanciful Kaisersaal with stucco work from F. J. Feuchtmayer (1708) is among the most beautiful banquet halls in Germany.

with the following highlights; the Kaisersaal (i.e. "Emperor Hall", stuccowork from Franz Joseph Feuchtmayer), the Prälatur (i.e. "Prelate's Quarters") with the Rococo study and the magnificently furnished library. Furthermore, there is a fire brigade museum in the east wing of the present-day palace. It portrays the development of fire-fighting with displays of historical hoses, devices, models and documents. The Bernhardusgang, connecting the south wing and the cathedral, was once a part of the abbey and was artistically embellished by the Wessobrunn stuccoworker Franz Schmuzer as was the summer refectory. The most renowned boarding school in Germany is located in the west wing. It was founded in 1920 by Prince Max of Baden. Its most famous pupil was the prince consort of Queen Elisabeth II of England. In the former farm buildings, visitors are afforded an insight into the historical working processes in art and pottery, manufacture of musical instruments, glass-blowing, gold and art metalworking, woodworking and cobbling in the arts and crafts village. Among the attractive sights to see in the 17 ha closed complex are the former royal stud, the Burs, the Gothic house with distillery museum, both gates and the Langer Bau (i.e. "long building", 1000 m² wine cellar, cooperage museum, Baumtorkel (i.e. "winepress") from 1706). The New Museum is reserved for changing exhibits. A large adventure playground, the pony farm and the playhouse for the little ones as well as a practice golf course, the abbey pub and the wine bar in the former prison round out the range of activities available for excursionists and vacationers on the palace grounds.

The greater community of Salem (pop. 10,000) consists of 11 town districts which offer a peaceful holiday stay away from the hustle and bustle. Recreational activities include hiking, bicycle tours and horse riding, as well as tennis, fishing and shooting, not to mention swimming in the spacious outdoor pool on the Schlosssee

▲ Abbey coin cabinet

Pony riding ▲

▼ Glassblowers   ▲ Salem Palace   Baumtorkel (ca. 1706) ▼

(i.e. "Palace Lake"). A charming drive (10 km) leads us up Salem Valley to the Heiligenberg and the climatic health resort of the same name (pop. 3100). The plateau at an altitude of more than 700 m affords visitors a splendid view out over the valley. Those here to spend time at the health resort and vacationers appreciate the clean air and tranquillity away from the busy traffic and tourist centres most of all. Active vacationers can pass their time on adventurous, marked hiking and bicycle trails, in a heated outdoor pool or playing tennis and miniature golf. In the wintertime, there are tracked cross-country skiing trails and two ski lifts in the town districts of Betenbrunn and Wintersulgen. Visitors can learn more about the indigenous plants and animals on guided hikes and bicycle tours with expert supervision. In addition to the cosy inns, the evening music performances

Construction of the Princely Fürstenberg Palace of Heiligenberg started in 1535 in Renaissance style where the medieval castle once stood.

Heiligenberg Palace. a magnificently carved wooden ceiling in Renaissance style, probably the most beautiful in Germany, spans the great Rittersaal.

and festivals of the local clubs also contribute to the positive vacationing atmosphere. Most health resort guests come here due to ailments of the respiratory tract; however, massages, medicinal baths and Kneipp applications are also administered, or the outdoor water treading facilities used by guests. Various forms of gymnastics and ball games offer welcome opportunities for exercise. The town's main attraction, though, is the Schloss der Fürsten von Fürstenberg (i.e. "Palace of the Princes of Fürstenberg"). It was built around 1575 at the site where a castle once stood on a jutting cliff on the steep slope. The lovely Renaissance palace was not once destroyed over the course of the centuries and was also hardly ever occupied, meaning it has experience almost no disturbing changes and is now considered one of the best preserved examples of this architectural period. The "Rittersaal" (i.e. "Hall of Knights") is the most famous. It is a 36 m long and 100 m wide banquet hall spread over two stories with a magnificent Renaissance ceiling made of carved wood overhead, probably the most beautiful of its kind in Germany. Precious carved furnishings also adorn the charming palace chapel. Both rooms can be seen on the tour as can the old living quarters from back then and the palace kitchen, which was in use until just a few years ago. From the terrace and the park of the Princely Fürstenberg Palace, you can see out to Lake Constance and beyond to the Alps with the Säntis on clear days.

The pilgrimage church in the neighbouring town district of Betenbrunn (3 km) is also worth visiting. It has valuable frescoes and a lavish Baroque interior.

Reichenau Island

Motorists can also return to the peninsula of Bodanrück from Meersburg with the car ferry Constance-Staad. The highway B33 leads along the south side from Constance in the direction of Radolfzell. After about 5 km, you reach the turn-off to Reichenauer Damm (i.e. "Reichenau Dike"). Nature lovers will want to take a side trip to the well-

tion centre is located in the former train station of Reichenau, which you can reach quickly by turning right at the intersection to the Damm. Visitors, who should come equipped with rubber boots, binoculars and, in the summer and fall, with insect sprays, have a good chance of spotting very rare bird species such as the king-

The Island of Reichenau: a modern sculpture of Bishop Pirmin; in the background is the Romanesque Church of St. George.

known Wollmatinger Ried (i.e. "Wollmating Marsh"), the largest area of marshes on Lake Constance encompassing 760 ha. To protect the birds that rest and brood here, the wildlife preservation area may only be entered within the framework of a tour, offered year round by the Naturschutzbund Deutschland (i.e. "Nature Conservation Union of Germany"). Its informa-

fisher, black-tailed godwits, black-necked grebes, and little egrets"). These are just some of the 200 bird species registered here in the marsh, roughly a third of which are brooding here. If you only have time for a brief visit to the marshes, turn off the B 33 about 1.5 km past the intersection in the direction "Waldsiedlung". You soon arrive at a fine vantage point.

Information

Verkehrsverein e.V. ("Tourist Association"), Ergat 5, D-78479 Reichenau, Phone 07534/9207-0, Fax: 9207-77
The churches of St. Mary and St. Mark, St. George and St. Peter and Paul are open for visitors during the day.
Treasure-Vault in the Cathedral of St. Mary and St. Mark: *May - September Monday-Saturday 11:00 AM - 12:00 noon + 3:00 - 4:00 PM.*
Museum of Local History: *May - September Tuesday - Sunday 3 - 5 PM.*

The road onto Reichenau Island leads over a dike since 1838, flanked by poplars to either side. On the way over, the Swiss shore on the other side of the Untersee is to the left, while the Gnadensee in front of the wide belt of marshes belonging to the wildlife preservation area is to the right. The wooded hills of the Bodanrück tower above the conservation area. We first pass by the prince-abbot fortification ruins of Schopfeln (10th cent.) and the modern sculpture of Bishop Pirmin, who founded Reichenau Abbey in 724. After passing the "Bruckgraben", we reach the island, known as the "Reiche Aue" (i.e. "Rich Meadowland"). Even though it is the largest island in Lake Constance, 4.5 km long and 1.5 km wide, it is still very manageable and easy for hikers and bicyclists

to explore. Today, the island is famous for both the Romanesque churches and the cultivation of quality vegetables, which now outstrips winegrowing and fishing. The industrious "Auer" (as the residents refer to themselves), profiting from the mild Lake Constance climate and the fertile soil, succeed in bringing in up to three harvests per year. The modern processing and harvesting machines and the numerous greenhouses, with electronically controlled temperature and humidity, go to show that the locals do not scorn state-of-the-art technology, either. On the other hand, the "Auer" successfully defy the construction of large-scale hotels on their 4.3 km² island. Instead, guests can look forward to cosy lodgings in small hotels, inns and holiday apartments as well as in

The Island of Reichenau, aerial view: from the left, the settlement of Niederzell, in the background, the dike to the Bodanrück and the Gnadensee to the left of that, in the foreground, the Zeller Lake, with the Untersee above.

private homes, accompanied by hearty local dishes as well as exquisite dining in a classy atmosphere. The bond to and rooting of traditions among the residents is also apparent from the number of clubs on the island, which is definitely unique in relation to the number of inhabitants. The appearances of the historically uniformed civic guards with their muzzle loaders and the local traditional dress groups are worth seeing. They appear in particular at the three special church festivals that only exist on Reichenau. At the festivals, the relic shrine from the treasure-vault of the cathedral is carried around.

The history of the once influential island comes to life in its three churches which belonged to the abbey in the Middle Ages. We come upon the first of these in the scattered settlement of Oberzell, dedicated to St. Georg. The Carolingian column basilica was built under Abbot Hatto III around the year 900, the Romanesque additions were built in the 11th century and the Gothic crossing was added in the 15th century. The church is famous for its extremely lavish mural paintings from the heyday of the abbey in Ottonian times (10th cen.). The half-length portraits of abbeys with books in their hands as a symbol of their official authority appear between the enormous round columns

Typical Reichenau: vegetable fields and the Romanesque Church of St. Georg in Oberzell.

St. Georg: Church of famous mural paintings (10th cen.).

Reichenau: Romanesque Cathedral of St. Mary and St. Mark in Mittelzell.

and the wide, spacious meandering friezes. The miracles of Christ are portrayed above in eight paintings, the healing of the sick and the raising of the dead. Below the mural paintings added at a later time, note the original portrait of "Geschwätz der Frauen" (i.e. "Women's Gossip", 14th cent.) which devils are writing on the proverbial "Kuhhaut" (i.e. "cowhide").

Following Seestrasse to the north-west, we soon pass the fish hatchery that contributes to maintaining the fish supply in Lake Constance at a high level in spite of intense cultivation. Finally, the street leads us to Mittelzell, where we once again meet up with Pirminstrasse, the main thoroughfare on the island. In the centre, we find the tourist office and the old city hall (14th cent., now a museum of local history) with the Gerichtslinde (i.e. "court linden tree").

A few minutes to the north, we come across the towering Cathedral of St. Mary and St. Mark. It is built on the location of the first church on Reichenau, which was founded in the 8th century together with the abbey by the itinerant Bishop Pirmin. He and some of his followers had a great influence on politics, architecture, literature, music and painting of the time in the 11th century, thereby leading to the renown of the large abbey. Abbot Waldo (786-806) was also the Bishop of Padua, Regent of the King of Italy and Chancellor of Charlemagne. He assisted the abbey school in getting a fine reputation as an educational institute of the elite and established the extensive abbey library, of which little remains today, though. His successor, Abbot Hatto I, friend and counsel of Kaiser Karl, functioned as his envoy in Constantinople and also as the Bishop of Basel. Walahfrid Strabo (838-849) was also one of the great abbots here. He enriched the imperial court in Aachen with his talents as a scholar, educator and poet. His garden book "de cultura hortorum", also known as "Hortulus", became famous. In the form of poems and rhymes, he describes the 24 cultivated plants which are tended to today in a new complex near the cathedral in the "Kräutergärtle" (i.e. "little herbal garden"). Abbot Hatto III even became the Archbishop of Mainz and Arch Chancellor of the Reich. The abbey had one last heyday at the end of the 11th century under Abbot Berno, who became known as the teacher of the later famous scientist "Hermann der Lahme" ("Hermann the Lame"), a universal genius in the areas of theology, mathematics, astronomy, poetry, music, and history. Soon thereafter, however, the importance of the abbey waned rapidly and became poor. From 1540, the bishops of Constance were also the abbots of Reichenau, before the pope dissolved the abbey in 1757.

The former abbey building in front of the cathedral was built just after 1600 and now serves as the city hall. The Romanesque church structure in its present form dates back to the 8th and 11th century: only the choir and treasure-vault are from the Gothic period. The west transept holds tombstones of abbots, a crucifixion ensemble (17th cent.) as well as the tombstone of Abbot Berno in the middle, and behind that the altar of St. Mark (1477) with the saint's relics and above that the Kaiser's Lodge, where the relics where once on display. The "treasure-vault" in the former sacristy with the Romanesque "Oberzeller Crucifix", five Gothic relic shrines and the ivory pyx (5th cen.) is especially worth visiting.

The former collegiate church of St. Peter and Paul in the town district of Niederzell is the last of the three Romanesque churches on the island. The present structure was completed around 1100 on the location of the basilica from the 8th century. The interior was modernised with a stuccoed Baroque vault in place of the flat ceiling. However, valuable Romanesque frescoes (start of the 12th cen.) were uncovered in the apsis of the nave: in the centre, Christ in the mandorla, surrounded by the symbols of the four Evangelists and the two patron saints of the church, in two rows below that, the twelve apostles and an equal number of prophets from the Old Testament.

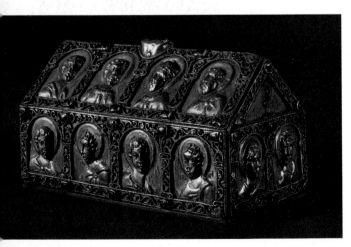

Reichenau: shrine of relics (ca. 1000) in the cathedral.

Reichenau: the two-tower column basilica of St. Peter and Paul in Niederzell was built ca. 1100.

In addition to its incomparable testimonies of a great historical past, Reichenau Island also offers today's visitors a wide variety of almost natural recreational opportunities: the range of recreational activities includes a sport boat harbour, surfing and sailing school, boat rental, beach, sport fields and tennis courts as well as well-tended hiking and bicycle trails, which lead up to the "Hochwart", the highest point on the island at 43 m above the level of Lake Constance. From this point, visitors have a far-reaching view of the island and out over the Untersee (Gnadensee in the north, Zellersee to the west and Rheinsee to the south). The town district of Reichenau-Waldsiedlung on the mainland is an ideal starting point for larger-scale hikes. As an alternative, you can set off on a ship excursion from the north (passenger ferry to Allensbach) and south (in the direction of the Rhine, to Mannenbach/Switzerland and in the direction of Constance) of the island.

Reichenau: a fisher repairs his nets. Cloister Mitterzell in the background.

Allensbach

On your way to Allensbach, it is worth making a short stop in the town district of Hegne, situated only about 1 km outside of Reichenau-Waldsiedlung. The Renaissance palace of Hegne once served as the summer residence of the bishops of Constance and has been renovated several times.

It has been used by the "Merciful Sister of the Holy Cross" as a provincial mother house for over 100 years. Many pilgrimages visit the grave of Sister Ulrika, who passed away here in 1913 at the age of only 31 and has been beatified since 1987.

Two kilometres down the road, we reach the

View of Allensbach, the Gnadensee and Reichenau Island from the Swiss shore of the Untersee.

Culture and Tourist Office, Rathausplatz 2, D-78476 Allensbach, Phone: 07533/801-35, Fax: 801-36
Museum of Local History: Pentecost through September Saturday 10 :00 - 11:30 AM, July/August, also Thursdays 10:00 - 11:30 AM. **Farm Museum in the town district of Langenrain:** information at 07533/6169.

village of Allensbach (pop. 6500), known in all of Germany as the headquarters of the Institute of Demoscopy (public opinion research). The town is over 1000 years old and served as a storage and loading point for the tax paid in kind in the Middle Ages, the "Zehnten" or tithes which the farmers dependent on Reichenau Abbey had to pay. Tradition has it that criminals who were sentenced to death were transported in the opposite direction, since all kinds of weapons were forbidden on the abbey island. The delinquents were executed on the gallows mount of Allensbach. If the "poor sinner's bell" of the abbey rung out during the crossing of the ship, then the convict was pardoned. He was released on the shore and expelled from the land. According to this tradition, this part of Untersee is known as Gnadensee (i.e. "Merciful Lake"). The Allensbach residents still demonstrate their historical connection to the island each year with the colourful "Water Procession" within the ceiling frescoes. The town can offer active vacationers well-tended lakeshore facilities, an outdoor swimming pool, boat, canoe and bicycle rentals, Kneipp facilities, tennis, fitness centre, sauna, solarium, and opportunities for sailing and fishing. Hiking enthusiasts will find this an ideal location: 85 km of marked trails lead, among other things, to a barbecue area and an instructional woods trail as well as to the wild animal and recreation park of Allensbach - with many animals that were once indigenous to the area - and to the rugged Marienschlucht (i.e. "Maria's Gorge") on the Überlinger See, which, however, belongs to the boundaries of Allensbach.

If you have planned a walk through the wild animal park, it is best to take the alternate route via Kaltbrunn to get onto the highway B 33 at the next Lake Constance village of Markelfingen. It is politically part of Radolfzell and is a popular resort town and starting

Allensbach: park grounds in front of the Baroque parish church.

framework of their Hometown Festival.
The half-timbered building of the old school (1751, today a museum of local history) and the Baroque church of St. Nikolaus are noteworthy historical structures here. The original Gothic church (15th cent.) with the onion tower is a sight that makes a pleasing impression with its lovely stuccowork and point for hikes on the Bodanrück. Sights to see here are the parish church of St. Laurentius (17th cent., mural paintings) and - about 2 km out of town - the Mindelsee in the middle of a wide belt of marshes. The region is a wildlife preservation area and can, therefore, only be entered accompanied by expert guides.

Radolfzell

A final bulge in the Gnadensee, the "Markelfingen Angle", begins at Markelfingen. Oppisite it is the Mettnau Peninsula, which is part of Radolfzell (pop. 28,000) and - together with Reichenau Island, seperates the Gnadensee from the Zellersee. On its north shore is the historic city centre of Radolfzell, as well as the landings and the

est treasure, however, is the early Baroque Rosenkranzaltar ("Rosary Altar", 1632) from the workshop of the Zürn brothers. The base of the "Hausherrenaltar" (18th cen.) contains the relics of Sts. Senesius, Theopont and Zeno, known as the "Hausherren" or "landlords". The first two members of the trio came to the then-fishing-

A view of the harbour entrance an dold city centre of Radolfzell.

yacht harbour, bathing beaches, boat hire stations, and the sailing and surfing school. The centerpiece of the old town is the Münnster "Unserer Lieben Frau" ("Saint Mary's Cathedral"), which was errected in the Gothic style starting in 1436 with subsquent Baroque modifications. It is to this spot that Radolf, son of an Alemanian aristocratic family and, as "Ratoldus", Bishop of Verona, supposedly retired in the year 826. He reputedly lived in a monastic-type "cell". His grave is inside the church. The church's great-

village with Radolf, the city's founder. The head of St. Zeno, who was likewise a bishop of Verona joined the other relics in the 11th century. Since at least 1542, the relics have been the focus of an annual solemn procession through the city in which, at times, as many as 20 surrounding communites have participated. The procession is also the start of a traditional festival know as the "Hausherrenfest", which also includes the "Mooser Wasserprozession", a procession of boats decorated with flowers. The Cathedral Treasury and the view

Information

Tourist Office, D-78315 Radolfzell, phone 07732/81500, fax 81510
City museum: Tuesday - Sunday, 3:00 - 5:00 PM; Wednesday 3:00 - 7:00 PM, Sundays and holidays 10:00 - 12:00 AM noon and 3:00 - 5:00 PM. *City Gallery* "Villa Bosch": Tuesday-Saturday 2:00-6:00 PM, Sundays and holidays 10:00 AM-12:00 noon and 2:00 PM - 6:00 PM. *Friedlinger Schlössle (between Radolfzell and Singen):* Open all year. Closed Mondays. Admission free. Phone 07731/43828.

Radolfzell: Cathedral spire ▶

▼ *MRadolfzell Cathedral:
Rosary Altar (1632, Zürn brothers).*

from the spire are also remarkable. At the marketplace in front of the cathedral, the"Ratoldus-brunnen" is a fountain commemorating the former bishop. The Österreichische Schlösschen ("Austrian Palace"), on the other hand, is a reminder of Hapsburg rule - with a relatively brief interruption during the period 1298-1806, when the entire area was accorded to Baden. The splendid building with its typical staggered gable was built starting in 1620 as the residence of Archduke Leopold Wilhelm; today it houses the city library. The stately "Reichsritterschaftsgebäude zum Georgenschild" (which is now the local court) is equally old, although it already evidences traces of the then inbreaking Baroque style. Between 1609 and 1805, this was the regular meeting place of the members of the Hegau Knighthood, who also had their administrative centre here. All the other noteworthy buildings are also grouped around the market and the cathedral: the city apothacary's with its pretty Baroque bays, the Gothic chapel of the Spital (16th cen.), and the Capuchin monastery, while the remains of the Medieval fortifications, including the three remaining towers and the modern park, mark the course of the city wall. At the Pulverturm ("Powder Tower"), one can exit the city gardens onto Seestraße. Here at the passage, bits and pieces of Radolfzell's oldest district, the "Griene Winkel" ("Green Corner"), have been preserved. It was once the preferred home of fishermen and farmers. At the north end of the city gardens, we reach a modern, glass-covered passage with many boutiques and little shops, but also the old Höllturm and the City Museum, the "Fürstenberger Torkel" (1389, owned by the Counts Fürstenberg since 1540), with its interesting coat-of-arms.

(literally, Scheffel's Little Palace") which poet Victor von Scheffel had built as a retirement home in 1878. To the east, the built-up area is seperated from the wildlife preserve by the Mettnau Wildlife Preservation Center. The wildlife preservation area encompasses 120 ha of meadows and marshes where hundreds of species of birds and also bats make their homes for at least part of the year. On the weekends, friends of nature can take tours with expert guides. Even from Floerickeweg, which leads from the sanatorium diagonally across the island to the Mettnauturm, you catch a glimpse inside. You can see even more from the observation tower itself, which affords a maginifcent panoramic view of the peninsula and parts of the Lower Lake that surround it. Another observation path is the"Naturpfad" ("Nature Trail") between Strandbadstraße and the Gnadensee. If you prefer contemplative walks in well-groomed parks, try the Istres Promenade and Mettnau Park, both of which extend along the "cultivated" shore of the Zellersees, where the city located its spa facilities starting in 1958.

The city spa and recreation centre, with sanatoriums, a spa centre, and a lakeside cafe, is in the Mettnau district on the peninsula of the same name. This is also the location of the "Scheffelschlössle"

Radolfzell: The Mooser Wasserprozession at the traditional "Hausherrenfest" in July.

Radolfzell: Mettnau Peninsula divides the Lower Lake into the Gnadensee (left) and the Zeller See. Reichenau Island is at the top.

The establishment of these facilities elevated it to the rank of a spa town for active therapuetic exercise.

For active vacationers, Radolfzell offers a broad palette of opportunities for engaging in the gamut of water sports, as well as hiking, bicycle touring, riding, and much more, even soaring and power boating. While the focus in the winter half of the year is on the traditional Alemanian Fasnet, the summer months are devoted to the aforementioned Hausherrenfest and the week-long musical events"Summer Academy" and "Summer Festival at the Band Stand", which also include plays.

Eleven km west of Radolfzell is Singen, the main town in the Hegau region, which borders Lake Constance to the west. The remnants of one-time volcanoes rise up out of the fruitful place like bowling pins. Formed during the Tertiary period, errosion has worn the formations down so much that today, only the former contents of the vents remain. In the Middle Ages, nearly all of these exposed vantage points, such as Hohenstoffeln, Hohenkrähen, and Hohenhewen (846 m) were fortified with castles. The most famous of the volcanic cones, which is also a Singen landmark, is the **Hohentwiel** (686 m). It offers a majestic view of Lake Constance and the Alps, and is also the starting point for a tour of Germany's most famous ruined castles.

The Höri Peninsula

Like a spearhead pointed at Reichenau Island, the Höri Peninsula juts out into the Lower Lake, separating it from the Zellersee. In the middle of the peninsula, the wooded mountain known as the Schiener Berg rises to a height of 708 m, separating the Lake Constance region from Hegau. Idyllic rural villages stretch out at its base, surrounded by orchards and fields in this ancient settlement-area.

The sometimes wide strips of shoreline between the towns, on the other hand, were largely left to fend for themselves. Today they protected as wildlife preservation areas. Today tourists benefit from them and from scenic hikes in the vicinity of the Schiener Berg.

The drive along the shoreway first takes us to **Moos** (pop. 2,800), which is famous for the historical water procession to Ra-

A view over Steckborn (Switzerland) and the Lower Lake to Höri Peninsula.

Tourist Office, Klosterplatz 1, D-78337 Öhningen, phone 07735/819-20, fax 819-30
Museum of Local History "Höri-Fischerhaus Wangen" in Öhningen:
April, May, September, October, every 1st and 3rd Saturday of the month, 2:30 - 5:00 PM; June, July, August, every Sunday 2:30 - 5:00 PM.
"Hörimuseum" in Gaienhofen: March - Oct., Tuesday - Saturday 2:00 - 5:00 PM, Sunday 11:00 AM - 6:00 PM.
Otto Dix House in Hemmenhofen: March - Oct., Wednesday - Saturday 2:00 - 5:00 PM, Sunday 11:00 AM - 6:00 PM.

Höri Peninsula: Half-timbered farm house (1839) in Bankholzen.

dolfzell that has been held every year since the vow of 1797 and the new homecoming festival known as "Bülle", which takes place annually in one of the city's districts and is dedicated to the red onions or "Bülle" grown in the region. Naturopath Franz Anton Mesmer (1734-1815) was born in the adjacent district of **Iznang.** His birthplace and a memorial room in the inn "Adler" are open to the public. Near **Horn,** a district of Gaienhofen, we have already reached the tip of the peninsula. Beside pretty half-timbered houses, the church, which is essentially Romanesque in style, is especially impressive due to its location on the lake and the lovely view. Inside, visitors can see a Rococo high altar from 1764 and two Gothic altar-wings. Due to their tranquil location on the lovely Lower Lake, the next two towns, **Gaienhofen** and **Hemmenhofen,** attracted an entire colony

of artists: chief among them were authors Hermann Hesse and Ludwig Frinckh, and painters Erich Heckel, Otto Dix, and Max Ackermann. Traces of their work may be seen at the Hermann Hesse House, in the Höri Museum (Gaienhofen), and at the Otto Dix House (Hemmenhofen). Gaienhofen Palace (built ca. 1700, today a boarding school) dates back to a castle that was owned by the prince-bishops. After the castle was modified, the Constance bishops' senior overseers lived here. In **Hemmenhofen,** the attractions include the handsome half-timbered buildings, the one-time Zehntscheuer or tithing barn, and the Sebastianskapelle ("Chapel of St. Sebastian", 18th cen.).
On our way back toward the Rhine, we pass **Marbach Castle,** which is located in a lovely park and evolved from an old castle that belonged to a robber baron.

An artist in his studio.

Otto Dix House: A basement mural.

Shortly thereafter we come to **Wangen,** another of the many small vacation spots on the lake. Today the oldest of its quaint half-timbered houses, the Höri fishermen's house (ca. 1600), serves as museum of local history. The exhibits here include artefacts from the age of the pile dwellings and fossils from Öhningen's limestone quarries. In **Kattenhorn,** the glass windows of the modern Petruskirche ("Church of Saint Peter") are a sight not to be missed. They were produced accord-

Hörl: Rose beds in front of the former Chorherrenstift in Öhningen.

Höri: Madonna of Schienen.

ing to designs by the expressionist Otto Dix and depict scenes from the the life of the church's patron saint. Furthermore, the little place has a castle that dates back to the 12th century and a Blasiuskapelle ("Chapel of Saint Blasius") from 1520.

The main locality of the largest of the three Höri municipalities, with 3,600 inhabitants, is **Öhningen,** another vacation spot in the vicinity of the Schiener Berg. Its Chorherrenstift (a religious foundation of Canons) was mentioned in official documents as early as 965 and became part of the Bishopric of Constance as a Provostry in 1255. The convent buildings originated ca. 1700. A precious Renaissance stucco ceiling has been preserved in the present-day parsonage. The choir stalls and elaborately carved Baroque figures have been preserved in the church. There are still a few historic 15th-19th century half-timbered houses in the town.

Another scenic route leads upward for 4 km toward the Schiener Berg. In the **Schienen** district of Öhningen stands the plain, Romanesque St.-Genesius-Kirche ("Church of St. Genesius", 11th cen.), a three-naved former monastic and pilgrimage church that originally had a flat wooden ceiling. Today the one-time provostry building (16th cen.) serves as the rectory. This makes an especially good starting point for hikes to the Schrotzburg ruins. From up here, as from other vantage points in this area, hikers enjoy a magnificent view.

A romantic Lake Constance sunset.

Stein am Rhein

An aerial view of the romantic town Stein am Rhein. Hohenklingen Castle is on the mountain slope; left of the Rhine is the Burg district of the city.

Information

Tourist Office, CH-8260 Stein am Rhein, phone 052/7412835, fax 7415146, international calling code from Germany: 0041.
Phonograph Museum: *daily 10:00 AM - 5:00 PM; guided tours by appointment.*
St. Georgen Abbey Museum: *March - October daily 10:00 AM - 5:00 PM, closed Mondays; closed on Good Friday.* **Museum zum Lindwurm:** *March - October daily 10:00 AM - 5:00 PM, closed Tuesdays.*

Stein am Rhein: picturesque row of houses on Rathausplatz.

It is 3 km from Öhningen to Stein am Rhein (pop. 3,000). At the halfway point, we cross the border to Switzerland; many of the areas on the right bank of the Rhine are in Swiss territory. Meanwhile, the Lower Lake has gradually narrowed again and the Upper Rhine starts at Werd Island. In earlier times, this was the closest point at which it was possible to build a bridge, approx. 25 km west of Constance. At this spot, which was favourable where strategy and transportation were concerned and which was already inhabited by pile dwelling builders 5000 years ago, the Romans maintained a bridge as a connection between the pacified Rätien and the often restless Teutons, securing it with a fort in the vicinity of the modern-day Burg district. A Benedictine abbey was founded here in 1005. The locality was soon granted the right to mint coins and hold markets and was chartered as a city in 1267. It became a free imperial town in 1457, a status it maintained until it joined the Swiss Confederation in 1484.

Many of the town's Medieval buildings remain largely unscathed by the passing years. For this reason, today the small town is one of the most visited tourist spots in Switzerland. It is sometimes (jokingly) referred to as "Rothenburg on the Upper Rhine", an allusion to the quintessential German tourist town. Besides the city wall with defensive towers and gate towers, Stein has numerous 16th and 17th cen. houses decorated with bays and frescoes. Most of them are arrayed around the picturesque Rathausplatz ("Town Hall Square") and its fountains, such as the pointy-gabled house "Vordere Krone" and the houses "Zum Hirschen", "Zur Krone", "Steinerne Traube" and "Zur Sonne". The frescoes on the house "zum Roten Ochsen", (Andreas Schmucker, 1615, scenes from the Old Testament and ancient mythology) and "Weißen Adler" are especially re-

Stein am Rhein, St. Georgen Abbey: Hall for Abbot David von Winkelsheim (1499-1525) with precious wall frescoes.

markable. The latter are the work of Thomas Schmid (16th cen.) according to motifs from the famous collection of tales known as "Decamerone". The Town Hall istself was built in 1539 and houses a historical collection with precious glass paintings.

Southeast of Town Hall, bordering on the bank of the Rhine, stands the former St. Georgen Abbey. Its present-day buildings are from the 14th - 16th centuries and are, for the most part, open to the public as a museum. Objects of particular interest include the hall and its lovely murals (1515/16) by Thomas Schmid and Ambrosius Holbein, the late Gothic refectories and apartments of the abbots, as well as the abbey and the former abbey church, a plain Romanesque basilica (12th cen.). West of Town Hall there is a puppet museum featuring more than 400 historical specimens of this popular genus of toy. On the left bank of the Rhine, the Parish Church of St. John, known for its lovely choir frescos (ca. 1400), rises from castle hill. It stands in the vicinity of the former

Roman fort (3rd cen.), the ruined walls of which have been preserved. From up here, visitors have a majestic view of the Medieval jumble of roofs. The village associated with the Roman fort was off to the east below the castle hill, in the modern-day district of Eschenz on the Lower Lake. Here is also Werd Island, where the first Abbot of St. Gall Abbey, St. Otmar, died in exile. The Otmarskapelle named after him has both Romanesque and Gothic walls. Today the island is connected to the mainland by a bridge.

Another Romanesque abbey church (11th cen.) survives in the suburb of Wagenhausen, 1 km west on the left bank of the Rhine. Opposite this, Hohenklingen Castle sits atop the mountain known as the Klingenberg, nearly 200 above Stein. In the 13th century, the castle was the residence of the minnesinger Walther von Klingen. Objects of interest include the collection of weapons and glass paintings from the 16th century. There is an especially splendid view from the precincts of the Medieval complex.

Stein am Rhein: The picturesque town hall or "Rathaus". built 1539-42, domi-nates the square known as "Rathausplatz".

Gailingen and Diessenhofen

On the overland route to Schaffhausen, we cross German territory again at Gailingen (pop. 2,700). First mentioned in an official record from the year 965, the town belonged to Canton Hegau-Allgäu-Lake Constance until 1806. The castle (ca. 1750) was built during this time. The oldest building in the town, however, is on Strandweg the district of Obergailingen: the Nikolauskapelle ("Chapel of Saint Nicholas", built 1100). Another object of interest is the Jewish cemetery estab-

lished in 1676 at the northern outskirts of the town. In the mid-17th century - with the permission of the lords of Randegg and the Austrian Hapsburg Superior Administrative Authority in Stockach - Jewish families settled in Gailingen. Around 1850, there were nearly as many Jewish members of the community as there were Christians.

In days of yore the town was characterised by farming and small-scale trading. Today it has modern clinic and rehabilitation facilities, and has advanced to become

View from Gailingen (Germany) to Diessenhofen (Switzerland). The covered Zollbrücke ("customs bridge") leads over the Rhine.

Responsible for Gailingen: Tourist Information, Haupstrasse 1, 78262 Gailingen, phone 07734/9303-20, fax 9303-50.
Responsible for Diessenhofen: Tourism Association, CH-8253 Diessenhofen, phone 052/6571077, fax 6573960, international calling code from Germany: 0041.

a state-approved spa in which the role played by fruit-growing and vinticulture is an ancillary one at best. All the same, however, Gailingen's high quality fruit brandies are also known throughout the surrounding region. Guests can avail themselves of bathing facilities at the indoor pool at the Jugendwerk or "Youth Centre" (evenings and weekends only) as well as in the young, clear Rhine (Rhein-strandbad), which, of course, is also suitable for fishing. Other leisure-time activities offered include skittles, tennis, and target shooting. Reading rooms at the tourist office and in the town library also offer vacationers the chance to use their time constructively. The same goes for the 80 km of paved hiking paths that lead again and again to grills with benches and scenic outlooks at the forest's edge.

The covered Zollbrücke ("Customs Bridge") leads in 10 minutes by foot to the former Free Imperial City of Diessenhofen (pop. 3,000). Lovely Gothic patrician houses and the remains of the medieval city fortifications (Siegelturm, 1545) have been preserved in the town, which has an antiquated feeling about it. Another highlight is the Parish Church of St. Dionysius, which was built around 1200 and modified in the Gothic style in the 15th century.

Just a few minutes below Diessenhofen by foot is the former Dominican Monastery St. Katharinental, which was erected in the 13th century and has been used as an old people's home since 1869. The late Baroque Monastery Church (1732-35) is considered one of the loveliest of this period in all of Switzerland.

Schaffhausen

From Gailingen it is only around 10 km to Schaffhausen (pop. 34,000), made famous by Europe's largest waterfall, the Rhine Falls. But the city itself, which is the capital of Canton Schaffhausen, is also certainly worth a visit, for much of its authentic cityscape has been preserved in authentic form. For this reason, we suggest a walking tour of the historic city centre, starting at the landing on the Rhine below Munot Fortress (where there is also parking available). Above us, the Romersteg leads us to the heights of the impressive fortress, a circular bastion in a strategically favourable, elevated position on the eastern city wall. The Munot was built 1564-1589, by which time the city already belonged to the Swiss Con-

Schaffhausen: A view from the Rhine up to Munot Fortress (16th century).

Tourist Service, Fronwagturm, CH-8201, Schaffhausen, Switzerland,
phone 052/6255141, fax 6255143,
international calling code from Germany (0041).
Munot: *May - September, 8:00 AM - 8:00 PM, October - April 9:00 AM - 5:00 PM.*
Allerheiligen Museum: *Tuesday - Sunday 10:00 AM - noon and 2:00 - 5:00 PM;*
May - October, Saturday and Sunday all day.
Hallen für neue Kunst: *May - Oct., Saturday 2:00 - 5:00 PM, Sunday 11:00 AM -*
5:00 PM. **Stemmler Museum:** *Sunday 10:00 AM - noon and 1:30 - 5:00 PM.*

federation (having joined it in 1501). The fortress battlements, which can be reached via the defensive tower, afford a majestic view of the city and the Rhine. A path known as the Munotstieg leads from the interior of the fortress, starting at the base of the defensive tower, back down into the lower part of the city. Here we turn right immediately and observe the Rococo building (Bachstr. 8), which was once the tavern of the guild of tanners. After crossing Bachstraße, we follow Goldsteinstraße to the left until reaching the grounds of the former "Kloster zu Allerheiligen" ("All Saints' Abbey"). Objects of interest here include a reconstructed herbal garden, the "Museum zu Allerheiligen" (collections from pre-history and the Middle

Fans of modern art will appreciate the "Hallen für Neue Kunst", a gallery opened in a one-time textile factory (south of the cloister at Baumgartenstr. 23).

North of the cloister district is Münsterplatz ("Minster Square"). In the western extension of this square we pass the Administration Building (a former armoury with a lovely portal) and come to another open square known as the Herrenacker ("Lord's Field"). Objects of interest here are the old Kornhaus or granary (1679), and the old Zeughaus or arsenal (lovely portal) next to the modern city theatre. From here, a narrow alleyway leads down to Fronwagplatz, the one-time marketplace. The Fronwagturm (today the Tourist Service building) collapsed in 1746,

Schaffhausen: The atmospheric Fronwagplatz was once the city marketplace.

Ages, departments for natural history and art with numerous rotating exhibits), the Romanesque minster (ca. 1100) with one of the loveliest spires in the Switzerland and, especially, the largest cloister in Switzerland, created in the 12th-13th centuries and evidencing both Romanesque and Gothic stylistic elements. It surrounds the "Junkernfriedhof" ("Squires' Burying-Ground"), where the local gentry found their final resting places between 1582 and 1874.

severly damaging the neighbouring Herrenstube (tavern of the local aristocracy, lovely portal) in the process. In the following year, both buildings were rebuilt in Baroque style. The astronomical clock on the tower is still the one installed in 1564.

To the west, the Obertor marks the former boundary of the city. The pretty Rococo facade of the house "Zum Steinbock" catches our eye in the row of houses in front of it. We cross Fronwagplatz, how-

▲ Schaffhausen: The Tellenbrunnen commemorates Swiss national hero William Tell.

▼ Historical personages on the patrician house "Zum Goldenen Ochsen".

▼ Schaffhausen: precious frescoes on the house "Zum Ritter".

ever, and pass two fountains. The upper one, called the "Mohrenbrunnen", was built in 1535 as a replacement for a wooden fountain. The building at Vorstadt 17 facing the former Rindermarkt or "Cattle Market" looks just as it did when built in 1606. It is an elegant patrician house with magnificent bay windows and portals as well as frescoes depicting the house symbol of a "golden ox" and personages of Mediterranean history. The Schwalbentor is at the north end of the street.

The Karstgasse starts opposite the house "Zum Goldenen Ochsen" and leads to the wide square or "Platz". The house at Platz No. 7 is a patrician house from 1746 with an opulent Rococo facade (trapezoidal bays, window crowns). Walking toward the Rhine, we pass the town hall and come to the Rathauslaube, in the second side street on the right, and the house "Zum Ritter", one of the loveliest patrician houses. The ornate

The Rhine Falls at Schaffhausen, the largest waterfall in Europe, is one of Switzerland's most interesting attractions. Especially in early summer, huge masses of water plummet thunderously up to 23 m into the depths over the 150 m wide falls. Two rocks have withstood the water's onslaught. The larger of the two has landings for boats and can be climbed.

painting on the facade was down by the famous local artist Tobias Stimmer in 1568 - 1570. It is the most important Renaissance fresco north of the Alps. Diagonally opposite this house is the mostly Gothic Parish Church of St. John (1248) at the former fish market, the modern-day Vordergasse. A little further eastward (at Nos. 28 and 26) stands a magnificent double house (1738) with a Rococo portal. The nearby Tellenbrunnen ("Tell's Fountain", 1522) commemorates Swiss national hero William Tell. From here, we haven't far to go until we again reach the starting point of our walking tour through the picturesque town.

Some 4 km upstream from Schaffenhausen, the waters of the Upper Rhine plummet thunderously up to 23 m into the depths over the 150 m wide falls, thus forming the mightiest waterfall in Europe. The panoramic view from the Hotel Bellevue is impressive, as is the view from the south bank of the Rhine near Laufen Palace, where viewers can follow landings to the "Känzeli" platform directly above the thundering falls. There is also a magnificent view from the restaurant at Wörth Palace (right bank). From here, small boats ferry visitors out to the larger of the two rocks, which can be climbed in total safety, in the middle of the waterfall.

The Rhine Falls at Schaffhausen:
An aerial view of the waterfall. The view from Laufen Palace (foreground) is just

as lovely as the one from Wörth Palace, opposite.

South of Rhine and Lower Lake

On the leg between the Rhine Falls and the end of this tour in Constance (46 km), we will stick to the southern bank of the Upper Rhine and the Lower Lake. In this area, the mountain slopes are very close to the water. The only habitable areas are those where tongues of land have formed at the mouths of brooks, such as at Eschenz near the mouth of the Lower Lake. The former castles Freudenfels, Liebenfels, Neuburg, and Glarisegg and the Klingenzell Probstei are witnesses to the strategic significance of the wooded lakeside ridge above the shoreways.

Nestled in orchards, the funnel-like mouth of the Upper Lake widens in the idyllic vacation spot **Mammern,** famous for the private clinic at Mammern Palace. It is situated in a lovely park with a stock of old and exotic trees. The Palace chapel is appealing due to its historical paintings

Steckborn on Lake Constance: Turmhof Palace (ca. 1320, towers and domed roof 17th cen.)

Information

Thurgau Tourist Information Office, Gemeindehaus, CH-8580 Amriswil, phone 071/4118181, fax 4118182, international calling code from Germany (0041)
Napoleon Museum in Arenenberg Palace: *All year: Tuesday through Sunday, 10:00 AM - 5:00 PM. For information, ring: phone 071/ 6641866, fax 6642513, international calling code from Germany (0041).*

and the beautiful organ. Nicely restored residences and excellent country inns contribute to the holiday atmosphere. Well-maintained hiking and horseback-riding trails lead to Neuburg (once the largest fortified stronghold on the Lower Lake), Glarisegg Castle, or the scenic outlooks at Hoch-wacht and Steinerner Tisch.

A series of historical buildings survive in the town of **Steckborn** (pop. 3600, charter granted in 1313). These include, besides the remains of the city wall and two defensive towers, the Town Hall (1669, with half-timbering and a tower-type staircase) and the Turmhof (1320) on the lake shore, the domed roof of which is fortified with delicate little spires. Today the building, which is also a city landmark, is set up as a museum. Exhibits on three floors include artefacts of the Neolithic and Roman periods as well as products made by famous local tinsmiths and master potters.

The city has plenty to offer in the way of recreation, with large parks and beach access, a modern yachting harbour, and many opportunities to pursue water sports or hiking. The little farming and fishing village of **Berlingen,** which is at the widest point of the Lower Lake, is characterised by houses set close together. Among those who have succumbed to the town's pastoral charm was the painter Adolf Dietrich (1877-1957), whose painting studio is open to the public.

The Sandeck Ruins and the palaces Eugensberg and **Arenenberg** follow one after the other on the slopes. Arenenberg Palace, in particular, has become famous as a **Napoleonic museum.** The outwardly plain country estate is located in the midst of a small park on a wide plateau above the town of Mannenbach. After Emperor Napoleon I was deposed (1815), even his family had to go into exile, including his adopted daughter and sister-in-law Hortense de Beauharnais. As the wife of Napoleon's brother Ludwig Bonaparte, she was Queen of Holland 1806-1810. In 1817, she bought Arenenberg Palace and furnished it according to her tastes. Her son, who later became

Ermatingen, former fishing village on a promontory on the Lower Lake.

Napoleon Museum in Arenenberg Palace: The private salon of Empress Eugénie (from 1873 on) of France.

Napoleon III (1852-1870), lived here at times, later with his lovely and influential wife Eugénia de Montijo. Above all, it was the two women who furnished the rooms according to their tastes and decorated them with exquisite works of art. In do-

Cherry blossom near Arenenberg, to which the families of both French emperors, Napoleon I and Napoleon III were exiled. On the other side of the Lower Lake is Reichenau Island.

ing so, Hortense was dominated by the austerity of the Empire, paired with French furniture of the High Classic era, furnishings in local Biedermeier style, and Romantic paintings. Eugénie refurbished her rooms in 1873, after the dissolution of France's Second Empire. She was attracted to the neo-Baroque style with flowery cloth wallpaper, intricate carvings and inlays, and Parisian castings. This was complemented by a collection of presents that the Emperor and Empress received from all over the world, as well as valuable paintings and sculptures. Thus the museum is in the fortunate position of being able to present the entire country estate of two generations of a 19th century imperial family.

A large tongue of land is occupied by the fishing village of **Ermatingen,** famous for pile dwellings discovered there and the ancient custom of "Groppenfasnacht", which is celebrated just three weeks before Easter. Attractions include picturesque half-timbered houses and fishermen's houses along the romantic alleyways, as well as the staggered gable of the church tower.

The local restaurants and their fish specialities bear witness even today to the community's close ties to the lake and its products. From nearby Wolfsberg Palace, hikers enjoy an excellent view over the Lower Lake all the way to Reichenau Island and the mouth of the Seerhein.

Two kilometres from Constance, on the Seerhein, is the one-time fishing village of **Gottlieben.** During the Council of Constance (1415), reformer Jan Hus, his companion Jerome of Prague, and one of three popes at that time, John XXIII, were held prisoner in the Constance bishops' palace (from 1251). Today the property is privately owned, but it is still an impressive sight when seen from the Seerhein. The idyllic location, lovely half-timbered buildings, hospitable hotels and restaurants, and modern water sports facilities make it a popular destination. In Constance, we reach the end of our tour of the Lower Lake.

Evening atmosphere on the Lower Lake near Mannenbach.

Lake Constance Customs

Although the eastern tribes, the Celts, and Romans had already settled at Lake Constance long before them, it is the Alemanians in particular who have made their mark on this region. Even today, they account for the bulk of the population, which speaks the unmistakably Alemanian Lake Swabian. The tradition that has been passed down with in the purest form is that of the Alemanian Fasnet (Mardis gras), which is usually celebrated between the Feast of the Epiphany and Ash Wednesday with balls and meetings of carnival associations. In many areas of Switzerland, carnival even continues until three weeks before Easter. Besides Karbatschen-Schellen (snapping whips), Alemanian Fastnet also includes the Narrenbäume (fools' trees) that are set up in the town on "Schmotzige Dunstig" (literally "dirty Thursday", the Thursday before Shrove

Tuesday), and the earthy masks ("Hemdglonker", "Hänsele", "Schnabelgiere", and the ever-present witches) that frighten or amuse visitors, especially on the last weekend of carnival. On Ash Wednesday, then, it is time to grieve. The Fasnacht is carried to its grave. Then the revellers meet in their favourite taverns for a meal of snails that marks the start of the fasting period. On the Sunday thereafter, the witches are burned. Tall bundles of wood and brush, fastened to a pole and decorated with a head and body, are burned in many places around Lake Constance. At festive events and parades, women and girls in particular often still wear traditional Alemanian costumes. Typical for this area are the precious lace bonnets which the women wear over the tight bodice with the scarf.

Alemanian Fasnacht at Lake Constance; Harbour revellers in Friedrichshafen.

▲ *Silvesterklaus from Urnäsch*

▲ *Weingeister of Trübbach*

▼ *Harbour revellers in Friedrichshafen*   ▲ *Überlinger Hänsele*   *Kornköffler in Lindau* ▼

Bündner Alpen

Schesaplana
2965

Falknis
2562
Augustenberg
2379

Calanda
2802

Piz
28

Graue I

Drei Schwestern
2052

Vaduz

Bludenz

Feldkirch

Altstätten

Lustenau

St. Margrethen

Rh

Dornbirn

Höchst

Fußach

Rhein Kan.

Hard

Fussacher Bucht

Pfänder
1064

▬ 9

Bregenz

▬ 10

W

Bregenzer Bucht

▬ 8

Lindau

Bad
Schachen

Was

Lochau

L. Reutin

L. Hoyren

Hörbranz